# About Math Connection:

W9-BBR-775

**W**elcome to RBP Books' Connection series. Math Connection™ provides students with focused practice to help reinforce and develop math skills in all areas defined by the NCTM (National Council of Teachers of Mathematics) as appropriate for sixth-grade students. These include numeration and operations, three- and four-digit addition and subtraction, probability, measurement, shapes, graphing, fractions, time, money values, word problems, multiplication, division, and decimals. Exercises are grade-level appropriate; with clear examples and instructions on each page to guide the lesson; they also feature a variety of activities to help students develop their ability to work with numbers.

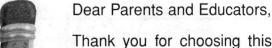

Dear Parents and Educators,

Thank you for choosing this Rainbow Bridge Publishing educational product to help teach your children and students. We take great pride and pleasure in becoming involved with your educational experience. Some people say that math will always be math and reading will always be reading, but we do not share that opinion. Reading, math, spelling, writing, geography, science, history and all other subjects will always be some of life's most fulfilling adventures and should be taught with passion both at home and in the classroom. Because of this, we at Rainbow Bridge Publishing associate the greatness of learning with every product we create.

It is our mission to provide materials that not only explain, but also amaze; not only review, but also encourage; not only guide, but also lead. Every product contains clear, concise instructions, appropriate sample work and engaging, grade-appropriate content created by classroom teachers and writers that is based on national standards to support your best educational efforts. We hope you enjoy our company's products as you embark on your adventure. Thank you for bringing us along.

Sincerely,

George Starks
Associate Publisher
Rainbow Bridge Publishing

---

# Math Connection™ • Grade 6
## Written by Laura Adams

Illustrations
Amanda Sorensen

Visual Design and Layout
Andy Carlson, Robyn Funk, Zachary Johnson, Scott Whimpey

Editorial Director
Paul Rawlins

Copy Editors and Proofreaders
Kim Carlson, Elaine Clark, Jerold Johnson, Linda Swain

Technology Integration
James Morris, Dante J. Orazzi

Publisher
Scott G. Van Leeuwen

Associate Publisher
George Starks

Series Creator
Michele Van Leeuwen

Please visit our website at
**www.summerbridgeactivities.com**
for supplements, additions, and corrections to this book.

First Edition 2003

For orders call 1-800-598-1441
Discounts available for quantity orders

ISBN: 1-932210-18-0

PRINTED IN THE UNITED STATES OF AMERICA
10 9 8 7 6 5 4 3 2 1

# Math Connection — Grade 6
## Table of Contents

# Addition Facts

Add.

Remember your facts!

1.
$$\begin{array}{r} 5 \\ +2 \end{array}$$
$$\begin{array}{r} 8 \\ +6 \end{array}$$
$$\begin{array}{r} 3 \\ +8 \end{array}$$
$$\begin{array}{r} 2 \\ +10 \end{array}$$
$$\begin{array}{r} 6 \\ +4 \end{array}$$
$$\begin{array}{r} 9 \\ +6 \end{array}$$
$$\begin{array}{r} 10 \\ +5 \end{array}$$

2.
$$\begin{array}{r} 8 \\ +9 \end{array}$$
$$\begin{array}{r} 6 \\ +2 \end{array}$$
$$\begin{array}{r} 4 \\ +8 \end{array}$$
$$\begin{array}{r} 2 \\ +2 \end{array}$$
$$\begin{array}{r} 9 \\ +10 \end{array}$$
$$\begin{array}{r} 2 \\ +3 \end{array}$$
$$\begin{array}{r} 4 \\ +4 \end{array}$$

3.
$$\begin{array}{r} 9 \\ +9 \end{array}$$
$$\begin{array}{r} 4 \\ +7 \end{array}$$
$$\begin{array}{r} 7 \\ +3 \end{array}$$
$$\begin{array}{r} 6 \\ +9 \end{array}$$
$$\begin{array}{r} 3 \\ +9 \end{array}$$
$$\begin{array}{r} 7 \\ +9 \end{array}$$
$$\begin{array}{r} 2 \\ +4 \end{array}$$

4.
$$\begin{array}{r} 7 \\ +5 \end{array}$$
$$\begin{array}{r} 3 \\ +5 \end{array}$$
$$\begin{array}{r} 6 \\ +8 \end{array}$$
$$\begin{array}{r} 8 \\ +4 \end{array}$$
$$\begin{array}{r} 9 \\ +7 \end{array}$$
$$\begin{array}{r} 6 \\ +3 \end{array}$$
$$\begin{array}{r} 9 \\ +8 \end{array}$$

5.
$$\begin{array}{r} 4 \\ +5 \end{array}$$
$$\begin{array}{r} 7 \\ +2 \end{array}$$
$$\begin{array}{r} 3 \\ +10 \end{array}$$
$$\begin{array}{r} 7 \\ +8 \end{array}$$
$$\begin{array}{r} 9 \\ +5 \end{array}$$
$$\begin{array}{r} 4 \\ +9 \end{array}$$
$$\begin{array}{r} 7 \\ +7 \end{array}$$

6.
$$\begin{array}{r} 9 \\ +4 \end{array}$$
$$\begin{array}{r} 8 \\ +10 \end{array}$$
$$\begin{array}{r} 7 \\ +6 \end{array}$$
$$\begin{array}{r} 8 \\ +3 \end{array}$$
$$\begin{array}{r} 2 \\ +9 \end{array}$$
$$\begin{array}{r} 10 \\ +4 \end{array}$$
$$\begin{array}{r} 3 \\ +3 \end{array}$$

7.
$$\begin{array}{r} 10 \\ +2 \end{array}$$
$$\begin{array}{r} 8 \\ +8 \end{array}$$
$$\begin{array}{r} 5 \\ +8 \end{array}$$
$$\begin{array}{r} 6 \\ +6 \end{array}$$
$$\begin{array}{r} 6 \\ +10 \end{array}$$
$$\begin{array}{r} 5 \\ +6 \end{array}$$
$$\begin{array}{r} 10 \\ +3 \end{array}$$

8.
$$\begin{array}{r} 2 \\ +8 \end{array}$$
$$\begin{array}{r} 3 \\ +4 \end{array}$$
$$\begin{array}{r} 5 \\ +5 \end{array}$$
$$\begin{array}{r} 6 \\ +5 \end{array}$$
$$\begin{array}{r} 5 \\ +7 \end{array}$$
$$\begin{array}{r} 7 \\ +10 \end{array}$$
$$\begin{array}{r} 3 \\ +7 \end{array}$$

www.summerbridgeactivities.com
Math Connection—Grade 6—RBP0180

## Addition Facts

Add.

Remember your facts!

| 1. | 7 + 3 = | 10 + 7 = | 9 + 3 = | 5 + 5 = | 4 + 3 = | 8 + 2 = | 10 + 6 = |
|----|---------|----------|---------|---------|---------|---------|----------|
| 2. | 6 + 6 = | 8 + 5 = | 2 + 10 = | 8 + 8 = | 3 + 3 = | 4 + 10 = | 9 + 2 = |
| 3. | 6 + 7 = | 10 + 8 = | 7 + 7 = | 9 + 4 = | 5 + 9 = | 8 + 7 = | 10 + 3 = |
| 4. | 4 + 2 = | 9 + 9 = | 3 + 6 = | 4 + 8 = | 9 + 7 = | 2 + 7 = | 5 + 7 = |
| 5. | 5 + 3 = | 8 + 6 = | 5 + 6 = | 7 + 4 = | 5 + 4 = | 3 + 2 = | 10 + 9 = |
| 6. | 4 + 4 = | 7 + 6 = | 9 + 8 = | 5 + 10 = | 6 + 9 = | 4 + 6 = | 8 + 3 = |
| 7. | 8 + 9 = | 2 + 5 = | 6 + 4 = | 4 + 7 = | 7 + 8 = | 2 + 9 = | 5 + 8 = |
| 8. | 2 + 8 = | 4 + 5 = | 7 + 2 = | 6 + 3 = | 9 + 5 = | 2 + 6 = | 3 + 9 = |
| 9. | 7 + 10 = | 4 + 9 = | 6 + 2 = | 2 + 2 = | 3 + 8 = | 7 + 9 = | 6 + 8 = |
| 10. | 9 + 6 = | 8 + 10 = | 7 + 5 = | 8 + 4 = | 6 + 5 = | 3 + 5 = | 5 + 2 = |

Math Connection—Grade 6—RBP0180

www.summerbridgeactivities.com

## Subtraction Facts

Subtract.

Remember your facts!

| 1. | 18<br>− 9 | 8<br>− 5 | 10<br>− 1 | 15<br>− 8 | 14<br>− 5 | 13<br>− 9 | 16<br>− 8 |
|---|---|---|---|---|---|---|---|
| 2. | 13<br>− 4 | 9<br>− 1 | 13<br>− 6 | 11<br>− 3 | 5<br>− 1 | 12<br>− 7 | 6<br>− 3 |
| 3. | 9<br>− 5 | 11<br>− 7 | 10<br>− 3 | 15<br>− 9 | 11<br>− 5 | 14<br>− 8 | 6<br>− 4 |
| 4. | 12<br>− 5 | 9<br>− 2 | 16<br>− 9 | 12<br>− 4 | 16<br>− 7 | 9<br>− 3 | 17<br>− 8 |
| 5. | 12<br>− 2 | 14<br>− 7 | 13<br>− 8 | 12<br>− 6 | 8<br>− 7 | 11<br>− 6 | 13<br>− 3 |
| 6. | 10<br>− 8 | 7<br>− 4 | 10<br>− 5 | 12<br>− 9 | 14<br>− 4 | 7<br>− 6 | 10<br>− 7 |
| 7. | 7<br>− 2 | 14<br>− 6 | 11<br>− 8 | 6<br>− 1 | 10<br>− 4 | 17<br>− 9 | 15<br>− 5 |
| 8. | 15<br>− 6 | 8<br>− 2 | 12<br>− 8 | 4<br>− 2 | 11<br>− 2 | 5<br>− 3 | 8<br>− 4 |

## Subtraction Facts

Subtract.

Remember your facts!

1.  $4 - 2 =$     $7 - 5 =$     $10 - 4 =$     $11 - 7 =$     $15 - 8 =$     $11 - 9 =$     $13 - 8 =$

2.  $10 - 8 =$     $9 - 5 =$     $12 - 5 =$     $18 - 8 =$     $14 - 5 =$     $13 - 6 =$     $12 - 9 =$

3.  $6 - 5 =$     $13 - 9 =$     $8 - 2 =$     $17 - 9 =$     $11 - 8 =$     $16 - 9 =$     $14 - 8 =$

4.  $15 - 6 =$     $7 - 1 =$     $9 - 2 =$     $12 - 4 =$     $9 - 7 =$     $8 - 5 =$     $7 - 2 =$

5.  $10 - 3 =$     $17 - 7 =$     $11 - 4 =$     $10 - 5 =$     $7 - 3 =$     $10 - 2 =$     $16 - 6 =$

6.  $12 - 6 =$     $13 - 5 =$     $10 - 9 =$     $16 - 8 =$     $6 - 3 =$     $9 - 8 =$     $11 - 2 =$

7.  $13 - 7 =$     $9 - 3 =$     $14 - 7 =$     $13 - 4 =$     $14 - 9 =$     $15 - 7 =$     $13 - 3 =$

8.  $8 - 3 =$     $18 - 9 =$     $9 - 6 =$     $12 - 8 =$     $16 - 7 =$     $11 - 5 =$     $8 - 6 =$

9.  $6 - 2 =$     $14 - 6 =$     $11 - 6 =$     $12 - 3 =$     $9 - 4 =$     $5 - 2 =$     $19 - 9 =$

10.  $8 - 4 =$     $12 - 7 =$     $17 - 8 =$     $8 - 1 =$     $15 - 9 =$     $10 - 6 =$     $11 - 3 =$

Math Connection—Grade 6—RBP0180
www.summerbridgeactivities.com

# Multiplication Facts

Multiply.

 Remember your facts!

| 1. | 6<br>x 4 | 3<br>x 1 | 9<br>x 7 | 8<br>x 3 | 7<br>x 7 | 5<br>x 8 | 6<br>x 7 |
|----|----|----|----|----|----|----|----|
| 2. | 2<br>x 3 | 6<br>x 9 | 5<br>x 4 | 4<br>x 9 | 6<br>x 6 | 9<br>x 8 | 5<br>x 9 |
| 3. | 8<br>x 8 | 2<br>x 5 | 1<br>x 4 | 4<br>x 6 | 9<br>x 5 | 3<br>x 7 | 8<br>x 6 |
| 4. | 4<br>x 7 | 7<br>x 5 | 2<br>x 2 | 5<br>x 1 | 7<br>x 4 | 8<br>x 9 | 6<br>x 3 |
| 5. | 8<br>x 7 | 4<br>x 3 | 5<br>x 5 | 4<br>x 2 | 9<br>x 6 | 4<br>x 8 | 3<br>x 5 |
| 6. | 9<br>x 9 | 1<br>x 6 | 7<br>x 9 | 6<br>x 5 | 2<br>x 7 | 7<br>x 1 | 9<br>x 4 |
| 7. | 5<br>x 6 | 8<br>x 4 | 5<br>x 7 | 8<br>x 2 | 3<br>x 3 | 6<br>x 2 | 1<br>x 8 |
| 8. | 9<br>x 1 | 6<br>x 8 | 3<br>x 9 | 7<br>x 8 | 4<br>x 4 | 8<br>x 5 | 2<br>x 9 |

## Multiplication Facts

Multiply.

 Remember your facts!

| | | | | | | | |
|---|---|---|---|---|---|---|---|
| **1.** | 9 x 1 = | 2 x 2 = | 3 x 4 = | 5 x 6 = | 7 x 5 = | 6 x 8 = | 1 x 5 = |
| **2.** | 7 x 3 = | 5 x 4 = | 8 x 6 = | 6 x 3 = | 2 x 4 = | 3 x 6 = | 8 x 7 = |
| **3.** | 4 x 3 = | 9 x 4 = | 1 x 7 = | 9 x 6 = | 5 x 2 = | 4 x 8 = | 9 x 7 = |
| **4.** | 6 x 6 = | 5 x 3 = | 9 x 8 = | 7 x 8 = | 8 x 4 = | 2 x 9 = | 8 x 5 = |
| **5.** | 3 x 2 = | 6 x 7 = | 4 x 5 = | 8 x 3 = | 5 x 8 = | 3 x 3 = | 5 x 7 = |
| **6.** | 9 x 2 = | 4 x 4 = | 8 x 9 = | 7 x 6 = | 2 x 8 = | 4 x 6 = | 3 x 7 = |
| **7.** | 1 x 3 = | 6 x 9 = | 9 x 3 = | 6 x 2 = | 4 x 9 = | 2 x 1 = | 9 x 9 = |
| **8.** | 8 x 1 = | 7 x 9 = | 3 x 5 = | 2 x 7 = | 7 x 4 = | 7 x 2 = | 6 x 5 = |
| **9.** | 6 x 4 = | 4 x 7 = | 5 x 9 = | 6 x 1 = | 8 x 8 = | 9 x 5 = | 8 x 2 = |
| **10.** | 5 x 5 = | 3 x 8 = | 2 x 6 = | 7 x 7 = | 2 x 5 = | 4 x 1 = | 3 x 9 = |

# Division Facts

Divide.

 Remember your facts!

1.    $1\overline{)9}$      $6\overline{)30}$      $9\overline{)81}$      $7\overline{)56}$      $4\overline{)24}$      $8\overline{)64}$      $3\overline{)6}$

2.    $8\overline{)48}$      $4\overline{)32}$      $6\overline{)6}$      $3\overline{)12}$      $5\overline{)35}$      $1\overline{)3}$      $9\overline{)54}$

3.    $9\overline{)27}$      $7\overline{)35}$      $9\overline{)63}$      $5\overline{)25}$      $2\overline{)4}$      $7\overline{)63}$      $4\overline{)20}$

4.    $8\overline{)56}$      $2\overline{)16}$      $5\overline{)30}$      $2\overline{)8}$      $1\overline{)5}$      $6\overline{)24}$      $9\overline{)36}$

5.    $4\overline{)16}$      $3\overline{)9}$      $7\overline{)14}$      $6\overline{)54}$      $4\overline{)28}$      $5\overline{)45}$      $6\overline{)36}$

6.    $5\overline{)40}$      $2\overline{)12}$      $1\overline{)7}$      $8\overline{)32}$      $9\overline{)72}$      $7\overline{)21}$      $8\overline{)72}$

7.    $9\overline{)18}$      $8\overline{)8}$      $4\overline{)36}$      $5\overline{)15}$      $3\overline{)18}$      $6\overline{)48}$      $9\overline{)45}$

8.    $7\overline{)28}$      $5\overline{)10}$      $3\overline{)24}$      $7\overline{)49}$      $4\overline{)4}$      $8\overline{)40}$      $7\overline{)42}$

# Division Facts
Divide.

Remember your facts!

1.  $25 \div 5 =$    $24 \div 4 =$    $8 \div 1 =$    $3 \div 3 =$    $18 \div 2 =$    $9 \div 1 =$    $36 \div 6 =$

2.  $24 \div 8 =$    $28 \div 7 =$    $63 \div 9 =$    $4 \div 2 =$    $16 \div 4 =$    $42 \div 7 =$    $15 \div 3 =$

3.  $12 \div 6 =$    $45 \div 9 =$    $15 \div 5 =$    $27 \div 3 =$    $72 \div 9 =$    $20 \div 5 =$    $72 \div 8 =$

4.  $49 \div 7 =$    $6 \div 1 =$    $14 \div 7 =$    $12 \div 2 =$    $42 \div 6 =$    $24 \div 3 =$    $56 \div 8 =$

5.  $10 \div 5 =$    $64 \div 8 =$    $48 \div 6 =$    $36 \div 9 =$    $16 \div 8 =$    $30 \div 6 =$    $32 \div 4 =$

6.  $4 \div 1 =$    $45 \div 5 =$    $14 \div 2 =$    $2 \div 1 =$    $24 \div 6 =$    $9 \div 3 =$    $18 \div 9 =$

7.  $27 \div 9 =$    $16 \div 2 =$    $30 \div 5 =$    $81 \div 9 =$    $21 \div 7 =$    $12 \div 4 =$    $40 \div 5 =$

8.  $6 \div 2 =$    $54 \div 9 =$    $40 \div 8 =$    $35 \div 7 =$    $5 \div 5 =$    $18 \div 6 =$    $56 \div 7 =$

9.  $48 \div 8 =$    $35 \div 5 =$    $8 \div 4 =$    $18 \div 3 =$    $20 \div 4 =$    $63 \div 7 =$    $21 \div 3 =$

10. $12 \div 3 =$    $36 \div 4 =$    $7 \div 7 =$    $54 \div 6 =$    $10 \div 2 =$    $32 \div 8 =$    $28 \div 4 =$

Math Connection—Grade 6—RBP0180          www.summerbridgeactivities.com          ©RBP Books

# Tips for Learning Multiplication Facts

Learning multiplication facts takes practice. There are many different ways to learn and remember them. Here are just a few tricks:

## Remember that multiplication is just repeated addition.

   is the same as

## Multiplication can be shown using equal groups or arrays.

$3 \times 7 = 21$

3 groups of 7    or    3 rows of 7

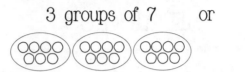 

## Make up rhymes, jingles, and mental images for the hard-to-remember facts.

5, 6, 7, 8;
So
56 = 7 x 8.

6 x 7 is 42;
Math is what I like to do!

## You can use the "double-double" trick to multiply with 4 as a factor.

4 x 7
is the same as
2 x 7 plus 2 x 7.

Keep doubling! You can also double a 4's fact to get an 8's fact.
8 x 7 is the same as 4 x 7 plus 4 x 7.

## You can double a 3's fact to find a 6's fact.

6 x 8 is the same as
3 x 8 plus 3 x 8.

## You can use your fingers to do multiplication by nines.

tens    ones

60 + 3 = 63

    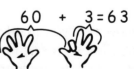

To multiply 7 x 9, count over 7 fingers. Bend down the seventh finger.

To get the answer, consider the fingers to the left of the bent finger as tens and the fingers to the right of the bent finger as ones.

For 7 x 9, 6 fingers to the left of the bent finger represent 6 tens, or 60. The 3 fingers to the right represent 3 ones. That's 63 in all. Try some other multiplications by 9 using this trick.

## Tips for Problem Solvers

How does a detective solve a mystery? A detective organizes facts and clues to solve a case. You can do that, too! A math student organizes facts to solve a math problem. Both the detective and the math student need to use various problem-solving strategies to help them.

> ## Problem Solving Strategies
>
> Draw a Diagram
> Use Logical Reasoning
> Look for a Pattern
> Guess and Check
> Use Objects/Act It Out
> Make an Organized List
> Make a Table
> Solve a Simpler Problem
> Work Backward

## When it comes to problem solving:

- Sometimes you may choose one strategy to solve your problem.
- Sometimes you need to use several different strategies.
- Sometimes your strategy will not work and you will need to try another one.

You will be given opportunities to be a math detective and practice your strategy skills in the pages ahead. Different strategy clues and hints will be provided on the Problem Solving pages to help you become a master problem solver.

# Pre-Test: Addition and Subtraction

## Add or Subtract.

1.
$$468 + 382$$  $$168 + 317$$  $$392 + 62$$  $$4{,}735 + 274$$  $$4{,}940 + 4{,}801$$

2.
$$747 - 324$$  $$6{,}008 - 37$$  $$883 - 69$$  $$2{,}066 - 275$$  $$9{,}385 - 5{,}673$$

3.
$$1{,}872 + 2{,}934$$  $$4{,}664 + 20{,}581$$  $$26{,}863 + 1{,}649$$  $$76{,}586 + 35{,}708$$  $$164{,}749 + 318{,}425$$

4.
$$8{,}604 - 7{,}238$$  $$5{,}657 - 3{,}948$$  $$9{,}400 - 2{,}848$$  $$4{,}006 - 2{,}378$$  $$6{,}300 - 4{,}677$$

5.
$$84{,}000 - 5{,}298$$  $$\begin{array}{r}5{,}138 \\ 7{,}824 \\ 3{,}205 \\ + 15{,}410\end{array}$$  $$28{,}000 - 6{,}243$$  $$\begin{array}{r}65{,}432 \\ 21{,}465 \\ 908{,}109 \\ + 258{,}738\end{array}$$  $$750{,}000 - 34{,}587$$

## Solve the equation.

6.    $c + 8 = 120$        $k - 6 = 13$        $j + 32 = 55$        $125 = n - 62$

## Solve each problem.

7. On Friday night, 37,589 people attended a concert. On Saturday 48,122 attended.
   a. How many more people were at the Saturday night performance?

   b. How many people attended the two concerts combined?

8. A large parking lot for an amusement park holds 2,000 vehicles. The parking attendant counted 219 empty spaces in the parking lot. How many vehicles are in the parking lot?

www.summerbridgeactivities.com                     Math Connection—Grade 6—RBP0180

# Addition

| Step 1 | Step 2 | Step 3 |
|---|---|---|
| Add the ones. Regroup as needed. | Add the tens. Regroup as needed. | Add the hundreds. |

Step 1
```
  1
7 9 6      6 ones
+ 1 7 5   + 5 ones
      1    1 ten, 1 one
```

Step 2
```
1 1
7 9 6      1 ten
+ 1 7 5    9 tens
    7 1   + 7 tens
          1 hundred, 7 tens
```

Step 3
```
1
7 9 6      1 hundred
+ 1 7 5    7 hundreds
9 7 1     + 1 hundred
           9 hundreds
```

## Add.

**1.**  
41 + 26  
324 + 452  
673 + 491  
82 + 471  
923 + 523  
357 + 193

**2.**  
518 + 276  
793 + 189  
437 + 825  
530 + 986  
28 + 507  
6429 + 2,538

**3.**  
351 + 1,768  
1,892 + 2,751  
3,576 + 763  
7,145 + 9,374  
1,482 + 4,209  
8,598 + 5,305

**4.**  
4,592 + 7,009  
3,572 + 6,490  
2,801 + 7,955  
4,921 + 3,038  
8,480 + 1,842  
4,426 + 3,557

**5.**  
28,465 + 37,879  
65,378 + 43,640  
18,647 + 23,755  
27,304 + 55,476  
21,450 + 74,607  
100,325 + 421,904

**6.**  
35,964 + 81,178  
36,832 + 22,597  
21,936 + 11,235  
41,874 + 32,297  
25,953 + 45,438  
584,767 + 222,354

Math Connection—Grade 6—RBP0180          www.summerbridgeactivities.com          ©RBP Books

# Column Addition

| **Step 1** Add the ones. Regroup as needed. | **Step 2** Add the tens. Regroup as needed. | **Step 3** Add the hundreds. Regroup as needed. | **Step 4** Add the thousands. |
|---|---|---|---|
| 5,446 2,339 + 7,628 ——— 3 | 5,446 2,339 + 7,628 ——— 13 | 5,446 2,339 + 7,628 ——— 413 | 5,446 2,339 + 7,628 ——— **15,413** |

## Add.

**1.**

| 82 | 46 | 186 | 266 | 452 | 547 |
|---|---|---|---|---|---|
| 28 | 27 | 355 | 275 | 397 | 218 |
| + 33 | + 35 | + 437 | + 123 | + 224 | + 193 |

**2.**

| 238 | 627 | 387 | 188 | 208 | 664 |
|---|---|---|---|---|---|
| 54 | 75 | 153 | 547 | 465 | 136 |
| 169 | 36 | 18 | 136 | 184 | 128 |
| + 115 | + 100 | + 434 | + 262 | + 922 | + 342 |

**3.**

| 1,644 | 2,345 | 3,651 | 5,246 | 1,565 | 3,437 |
|---|---|---|---|---|---|
| 1,065 | 1,127 | 2,048 | 3,254 | 1,040 | 2,059 |
| + 2,099 | + 2,269 | + 1,192 | + 2,108 | + 2,371 | + 3,128 |

**4.**

| 2,568 | 1,308 | 3,724 | 8,246 | 3,975 | 6,572 |
|---|---|---|---|---|---|
| 2,643 | 6,794 | 5,281 | 1,766 | 8,215 | 3,225 |
| + 2,345 | + 2,142 | + 1,723 | + 4,078 | 1,246 | 4,257 |
|  |  |  |  | + 4,078 | + 9,219 |

**5.**

| 41,238 | 15,724 | 32,264 | 56,124 | 32,617 | 18,399 |
|---|---|---|---|---|---|
| 32,642 | 71,283 | 40,272 | 21,432 | 92,647 | 53,478 |
| + 68,392 | + 28,239 | + 14,718 | 39,789 | 76,313 | 12,122 |
|  |  |  | + 28,895 | + 64,624 | + 36,547 |

# Subtraction

| Step 1 | Step 2 | Step 3 |
|---|---|---|
| Subtract the ones. Regroup as needed. | Subtract the tens. Regroup as needed. | Subtract the hundreds. |

Step 1:
$$\begin{array}{r} 35\,\overset{4\,|18}{\cancel{5}\,\cancel{8}} \\ -18\,9 \\ \hline 9 \end{array}$$ 5 tens as 4 tens, 10 ones.

Step 2:
$$\begin{array}{r} \overset{2\,|14\,|18}{\cancel{3}\,\cancel{5}\,\cancel{8}} \\ -1\,8\,9 \\ \hline 6\,9 \end{array}$$ 3 hundreds as 2 hundreds, 10 tens.

Step 3:
$$\begin{array}{r} \overset{2\,|14\,18}{\cancel{3}\,\cancel{5}\,\cancel{8}} \\ -1\,8\,9 \\ \hline 1\,6\,9 \end{array}$$

**Remember:** 18 ones is the same as 1 ten, 8 ones.

## Subtract.

**1.**

| 285 | 478 | 871 | 119 | 663 | 487 |
|---|---|---|---|---|---|
| − 162 | − 256 | − 557 | − 54 | − 49 | − 138 |

**2.**

| 852 | 579 | 265 | 565 | 726 | 419 |
|---|---|---|---|---|---|
| − 451 | − 498 | − 77 | − 178 | − 329 | − 287 |

**3.**

| 394 | 267 | 744 | 128 | 764 | 672 |
|---|---|---|---|---|---|
| − 263 | − 119 | − 498 | − 68 | − 332 | − 579 |

**4.**

| 7,462 | 6,295 | 7,221 | 3,936 | 1,111 | 8,347 |
|---|---|---|---|---|---|
| − 189 | − 2,174 | − 5,321 | − 2,878 | − 674 | − 1,358 |

**5.**

| 9,311 | 5,322 | 9,435 | 4,254 | 2,414 | 4,592 |
|---|---|---|---|---|---|
| − 781 | − 693 | − 1,634 | − 2,965 | − 923 | − 1,497 |

**6.**

| 1,983 | 8,214 | 3,465 | 37,235 | 92,136 | 641,308 |
|---|---|---|---|---|---|
| − 1,288 | − 5,321 | − 2,877 | − 16,879 | − 48,657 | − 212,715 |

# Addition and Subtraction Problem Solving

Use the data in the table to solve each problem.

| City | Population in 2000 | Tallest Building | Height of Building |
|------|--------------------|-----------------|--------------------|
| Boston | 589,141 | John Hancock Tower | 790 feet |
| Chicago | 2,896,016 | Sears Tower | 1,450 feet |
| Denver | 554,445 | Republic Plaza | 714 feet |
| San Francisco | 776,773 | Transamerica Pyramid | 853 feet |

How many people live in Denver and San Francisco altogether?
**Think:** There are 554,445 people living in Denver and 776,773 people living in San Francisco. To find the total number of people living in both cities, you need to add.

$$\begin{array}{r} 554,445 \\ +776,773 \\ \hline \mathbf{1,331,218} \end{array}$$

So there are 1,331,218 people living in both cities.

1. How many more people lived in Boston than in Denver in 2000?

    Do you need to add, subtract, or both? _____

2. What was the total population of Boston and Chicago in 2000?

    Do you need to add, subtract, or both? _____

3. How many more people live in the two cities with the largest population than the two cities with the smallest population?

    Do you need to add, subtract, or both? _____

4. How much taller is the Transamerica Pyramid than the John Hancock Tower?

    Do you need to add, subtract, or both? _____

5. How much taller is the tallest building listed than the shortest one?

    Do you need to add, subtract, or both? _____

6. If all four of the buildings in the data table were stacked on top of each other, how tall would they be?

    Do you need to add, subtract, or both? _____

# Subtracting across Zeros

| **Step 1** Subtract the ones. Regroup as needed. | **Step 2** Subtract the tens. | **Step 3** Subtract the hundreds. | **Step 4** Subtract the thousands. |
|---|---|---|---|
| $$\begin{array}{r} {}^{9}\ {}^{9} \\ {}^{1}\,{}^{10}{}^{10}{}^{11} \\ 2,0\;0\;1 \\ -\quad1\;4\;8 \\ \hline 3 \end{array}$$ Not enough ones, tens, or hundreds. Regroup thousands. <br> 1,000 is 10 hundreds. 100 is 10 tens. | $$\begin{array}{r} {}^{9}\ {}^{9} \\ {}^{1}\,{}^{10}{}^{10}{}^{11} \\ 2,0\;0\;1 \\ -\quad1\;4\;8 \\ \hline 5\;3 \end{array}$$ | $$\begin{array}{r} {}^{9}\ {}^{9} \\ {}^{1}\,{}^{10}{}^{10}{}^{11} \\ 2,0\;0\;1 \\ -\quad1\;4\;8 \\ \hline 8\;5\;3 \end{array}$$ | $$\begin{array}{r} {}^{9}\ {}^{9} \\ {}^{1}\,{}^{10}{}^{10}{}^{11} \\ 2,0\;0\;1 \\ -0\;1\;4\;8 \\ \hline 1,8\;5\;3 \end{array}$$ Write in **0** if it helps you. |

## Subtract.

| | | | | | |
|---|---|---|---|---|---|
| **1.** 500 <br> − 324 | 7,000 <br> − 4,968 | 300 <br> − 136 | 4,001 <br> − 1,292 | 8,000 <br> − 4,449 | 2,000 <br> − 376 |
| **2.** 6,006 <br> − 723 | 3,300 <br> − 1,551 | 5,900 <br> − 899 | 4,003 <br> − 423 | 6,010 <br> − 2,087 | 7,040 <br> − 2,634 |
| **3.** 7,003 <br> − 298 | 6,010 <br> − 3,478 | 4,000 <br> − 298 | 1,303 <br> − 797 | 9,070 <br> − 3,559 | 3,005 <br> − 2,228 |
| **4.** 80,700 <br> − 2,859 | 58,000 <br> − 1,846 | 36,000 <br> − 3,582 | 95,000 <br> − 7,432 | 89,000 <br> − 14,832 | 45,000 <br> − 16,548 |
| **5.** 40,000 <br> − 15,972 | 90,000 <br> − 30,421 | 350,000 <br> − 4,561 | 210,050 <br> − 8,993 | 700,600 <br> − 68,758 | 500,100 <br> − 24,152 |
| **6.** 400,000 <br> − 27,764 | 800,000 <br> − 28,828 | 100,000 <br> − 9,999 | 200,000 <br> − 7,147 | 700,000 <br> − 28,282 | 600,000 <br> − 66,666 |

Math Connection—Grade 6—RBP0180   www.summerbridgeactivities.com   ©RBP Books

## Addition and Subtraction Practice

Solve each problem in the pyramid. Add up all your answers in the spaces provided below. What is the sum of all the numbers?

 Hint: Break this problem up into smaller sums. Then add together the smaller sums to get the total sum.

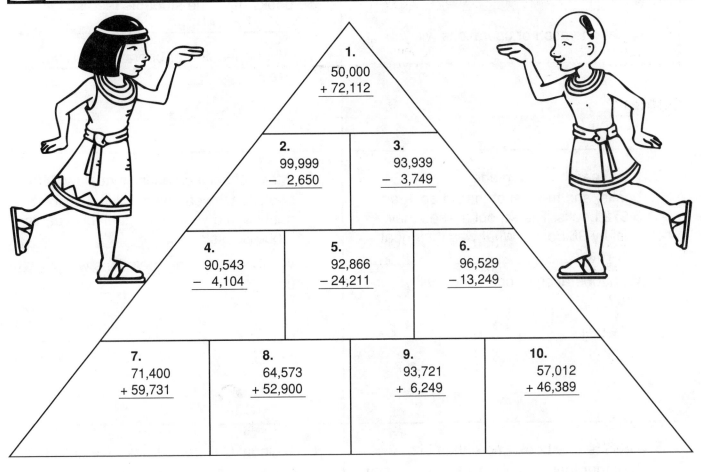

1.
50,000
+ 72,112

2.
99,999
−  2,650

3.
93,939
−  3,749

4.
90,543
−  4,104

5.
92,866
− 24,211

6.
96,529
− 13,249

7.
71,400
+ 59,731

8.
64,573
+ 52,900

9.
93,721
+  6,249

10.
57,012
+ 46,389

1. _____

2. _____

3. _____

4. _____

5. _____

6. _____

7. _____

8. _____

9. _____

10. _____

= _____ **Total**

# Addition and Subtraction Problem Solving

Solve each problem.

1. The sixth graders of Jackson Elementary School want to read 1,000 books for their school's annual Read-A-Thon. So far they have read 617. How many more books do they need to read to reach their goal?

   _____

   What operation or operations will you use? _____

2. This year, the Jackson Elementary schoolwide goal for the Read–A–Thon is 7,000 books. The librarian told the students they need to read 1,308 more books to reach their goal. How many books have the students read so far?

   _____

   What operation or operations will you use? _____

3. Last year the sixth graders read 682 books, and the rest of the school read 5,972 books. The school missed their goal by 96 books. What was their goal last year? _____

   What operation or operations will you use? _____

4. If the school increases its goal by 250 books each year, what will the school's goal be in 5 years if its goal this year is 7,000 books? _____

   What operation or operations will you use? _____

5. Kevin read 9 books more than Liz. Together they read 43 books. How many books did Liz read? _____

   What operation or operations will you use? _____

6. National Children's Book Week takes place the third week of November. It was first held in 1919. As of November 2002, how many years had it been celebrated so far? _____

   What operation or operations will you use? _____

## Solving Addition Equations

An algebraic equation contains **numbers**, **variables**, **operations**, and an **equal sign**.

In the equation **$x + 3 = 10$**, **x** is the variable and **+** is the operation.
This equation means that some number (we'll call it $x$) plus 3 is equal to 10.

Remember that a variable is a letter that stands for an unknown number.

Solve: $t + 6 = 9$

1. **Think:** What number plus 6 is equal to 9?     $t + 6 = 9$    Subtraction is the inverse of addition.
2. Choose the inverse operation:
   Subtract 6 from the other side of the equation.    $t = 9 - 6$
3. Simplify.    $t = 3$
4. Check your solution.
   Substitute 3 for $t$ to see if the equation is true.    $t + 6 = 9$    The equation is
      $\mathbf{3} + 6 = 9$    true, so the
      $9 = 9$    solution is correct.

### Complete the steps and find the solutions to the equations.

1.
$x + 8 = 12$      $7 + a = 18$      $z + 6 = 14$
$x = 12 - \underline{\mathbf{8}}$      $a = 18 - \underline{\phantom{00}}$      $z = 14 - \underline{\phantom{00}}$
$x = \underline{\mathbf{4}}$      $a = \underline{\phantom{00}}$      $z = \underline{\phantom{00}}$

2.
$7 + j = 15$      $k + 5 = 20$      $7 + p = 16$
$j = 15 - \underline{\phantom{00}}$      $k = 20 - \underline{\phantom{00}}$      $p = 16 - \underline{\phantom{00}}$
$j = \underline{\phantom{00}}$      $k = \underline{\phantom{00}}$      $p = \underline{\phantom{00}}$

### Solve the equations.

3.    $y + 8 = 11$      $x + 8 = 24$      $v + 3 = 13$      $m + 12 = 18$

4.    $c + 7 = 13$      $n + 6 = 18$      $h + 9 = 27$      $s + 16 = 32$

5.    $a + 7 = 20$      $8 + w = 17$      $g + 15 = 31$      $8 + p = 26$

## Solving Subtraction Equations

Solve: $y - 8 = 9$

1. **Think:** What number minus 8 is equal to 9?　　　$y - 8 = 9$　　Addition is the inverse of subtraction.

2. Choose the inverse operation:
   Add 8 to the other side of the equation.　　$y = 9 + 8$

3. Simplify.　　　　　　　　　　　　　　　　$y = 17$

4. Check your solution.　　　　　　　　　　　$y - 8 = 9$　　The equation is true, so the solution is correct.
   Substitute 17 for $y$ to see if the equation is true.　**17** $- 8 = 9$
   　　　　　　　　　　　　　　　　　　　　　$9 = 9$

### Complete the steps and find the solutions to the equations.

**1.**
$$x - 6 = 5$$
$$x = 5 + \underline{\textbf{6}}$$
$$x = \underline{\textbf{11}}$$

$$n - 8 = 7$$
$$n = 7 + \underline{\phantom{xx}}$$
$$n = \underline{\phantom{xx}}$$

$$y - 8 = 13$$
$$y = 13 + \underline{\phantom{xx}}$$
$$y = \underline{\phantom{xx}}$$

**2.**
$$h - 25 = 17$$
$$h = 17 + \underline{\phantom{xx}}$$
$$h = \underline{\phantom{xx}}$$

$$k - 62 = 125$$
$$k = 125 + \underline{\phantom{xx}}$$
$$k = \underline{\phantom{xx}}$$

$$100 = p - 20$$
$$100 + \underline{\phantom{xx}} = p$$
$$\underline{\phantom{xx}} = p$$

### Solve the equations.

**3.**　　$g - 19 = 37$　　　　$x - 9 = 27$　　　　$j - 10 = 16$　　　　$m - 8 = 20$

**4.**　　$q - 15 = 100$　　　$r - 19 = 37$　　　$w - 32 = 32$　　　$z - 12 = 29$

**5.**　　$y - 122 = 45$　　　$h - 25 = 0$　　　　$a - 16 = 20$　　　$c - 83 = 24$

**6.**　　$52 = j - 19$　　　　$41 = f - 10$　　　$17 = d - 105$　　$31 = n - 11$

Math Connection—Grade 6—RBP0180　　　　www.summerbridgeactivities.com　　　©RBP Books

# Post-test: Addition and Subtraction

Add or subtract.

1.
| 208 | 320 | 731 | 8,653 | 4,684 |
|-----|-----|-----|-------|-------|
| + 34 | + 413 | + 6,855 | + 272 | + 4,327 |

2.
| 678 | 921 | 840 | 6,795 | 7,428 |
|-----|-----|-----|-------|-------|
| − 223 | − 68 | − 252 | − 486 | − 6,274 |

3.
| 2,489 | 36,683 | 84,315 | 956,576 | 54,700 |
|-------|--------|--------|---------|--------|
| + 12,975 | + 1,024 | + 79,549 | + 137,142 | 23,405 |
| | | | | 43,617 |
| | | | | + 56,252 |

4.
| 9,242 | 45,572 | 72,510 | 95,853 | 400,000 |
|-------|--------|--------|--------|---------|
| − 3,784 | − 9,784 | − 18,982 | − 61,963 | − 24,351 |

## Solve the equations.

5.  $y + 7 = 16$    $x - 62 = 125$    $k + 5 = 20$    $17 = y - 25$

## Solve each problem.

6. The Cool Kid Computer Company produced 570,237 computer games during the first half of the year and 625,710 computer games during the last half of the year.
   a. How many more games did it produce during the last half of the year? _____
   b. How many computer games did it produce altogether during the entire year?

   _____

7. Greg kept a record of the number of hits to his web site during the month of February. The first week he had 1,187 hits. The second week he had 745. The third week he had 2,132, and the fourth week he had 3,521. How many hits did he have altogether during February?

   _____

## Standard Measurement: Units of Length

The chart shows the relationship between units of length in the Customary Measurement System.

Divide to change a smaller unit to a larger unit.
51 feet = ___ yards
**Think:** 3 ft. = 1 yd.
    51 ÷ 3 = 17
    51 ft. = 17 yd.

Multiply to change a larger unit to a smaller unit.
6 yards = ___ inches
**Think:** 1 yd. = 36 in.
    6 x 36 = 216
    6 yd. = 216 in.

| **Units of Length** | |
| --- | --- |
| 12 inches (in.) | = 1 foot (ft.) |
| 3 feet | = 1 yard (yd.) |
| 36 inches | = 1 yard |
| 5,280 feet | = 1 mile (mi.) |
| 1,760 yards | = 1 mile |

## Circle the greater length.

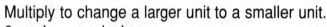

1.  10 in.  or  1 ft.        3 ft.  or  38 in.        1 ft. 7 in.  or  17 in.

2.  4 ft. 4 in.  or  56 in.        1 ft. 9 in.  or  2 ft.        7 ft.  or  2 yd.

3.  6 yd.  or  17 ft.        26 in.  or  2 ft.        5 ft.  or  $1\frac{1}{2}$ yd.

4.  110 in.  or  3 yd.        5,000 ft.  or  1 mi.        11,000 ft.  or  2 mi.

5.  5,000 yd.  or  3 mi.        7,020 ft.  or  4 mi.        3,200 yd.  or  2 mi.

## Write the equivalent measure.

6.  6 ft. = _____ in.        72 in. = _____ yd.        2 mi. = _____ yd.

7.  24 in. = _____ ft.        18 ft. = _____ yd.        $1\frac{1}{2}$ ft. = _____ in.

8.  12 in. = _____ yd.        2 mi. = _____ ft.        1 ft. 3 in. = _____ in.

9.  1 yd. 11 in. = _____ in.        4 yd. = _____ ft.        $\frac{2}{3}$ yd. = _____ ft.

10.  60 in. = _____ ft.        5,280 yd. = _____ mi.        10 yd. = _____ in.

11.  10 mi. = _____ yd.        8 ft. 12 in. = _____ yd.        1 mi. = _____ ft.

# Standard Measurement: Units of Capacity

The amount of liquid a container can hold can be measured by using units such as the cup and the quart.

Many of the bottled liquids you buy in the store are measured in fluid ounces (fl. oz.). There are 8 fluid ounces in a cup, 16 fluid ounces in a pint, 32 fluid ounces in a quart, and 128 fluid ounces in a gallon.

| Units of Capacity | |
|---|---|
| 8 fluid ounces (fl. oz.) | = 1 cup (c) |
| 2 cups | = 1 pint (pt.) |
| 16 fluid ounces | = 1 pint |
| 2 pints | = 1 quart (qt.) |
| 4 quarts | = 1 gallon (gal.) |

**Examples:**

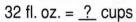

32 fl. oz. = _?_ cups
**Think:** 1 c = 8 fl. oz. To change from a smaller unit to a larger unit, <u>divide</u>.
32 ÷ 8 = 4      32 fl. oz. = 4 c

5 qt. = _?_ pt.
**Think:** 1 qt. = 2 pt. To change from a larger unit to a smaller unit, <u>multiply</u>.
5 x 2 = 10
5 qt. = 10 pt.

## Choose the most reasonable unit of measure for each.

Write **fl. oz.**, **c**, **pt.**, **qt.**, or **gal.**

**1.**  a can of soda _____     a pitcher of juice _____     a drop of water _____

**2.**  the water in a bathtub _____     the amount of sugar in a cake recipe _____

## Write the equivalent measure.

**3.**  1 qt. = _____ pt.          32 fl. oz. = _____ c          2 c = _____ pt.

**4.**  16 fl. oz. = _____ pt.     3 gal. = _____ qt.            1 pt. = _____ fl. oz.

**5.**  $\frac{1}{2}$ gal. = _____ c        $\frac{1}{2}$ gal. = _____ pt.       $\frac{1}{2}$ gal. = _____ qt.

**6.**  3 qt. = _____ pt.          4 pt. = _____ gal.            1 gal. = _____ fl. oz.

**7.**  8 gal. = _____ qt.         12 qt. = _____ gal.           22 pt. = _____ qt.

## Compare. Use <, >, or =.

**8.**  10 fl. oz. _____ 1 c       5 qt. _____ 2 gal.            2 c _____ 46 fl. oz.

**9.**  64 fl. oz. _____ 2 qt.     3 gal. _____ 22 pt.           12 pt. _____ 3 gal.

**10.**  160 fl. oz. _____ 10 pt.  100 fl. oz. _____ 10 c        100 qt. _____ 125 gal.

## Standard Measurement: Units of Weight

The basic unit of weight in the Customary Measurement System is the **pound**.
- Four sticks of butter weigh 1 pound.
- A large truck weighs about 2 tons.

**Remember:**
To change from a smaller unit to a larger unit, divide. To change from a larger unit to a smaller unit, multiply.

**Example:**
64 oz. = _?_ lb.
**Think:** 1 lb. = 16 oz.
64 ÷ 16 = 4
64 oz. = 4 lb.

**Units of Weight**
16 ounces (oz.) = 1 pound (lb.)
2,000 pounds = 1 ton

### Write the equivalent weight.

1. 96 oz. = _____ lb.      3 lb. = _____ oz.      7 tons = _____ lb.

2. 1 ton = _____ oz.      160 oz. = _____ lb.      10,000 lb. = _____ tons

3. 16 lb. 5 oz. = _____ oz.      9 lb. 3 oz. = _____ oz.      $2\frac{1}{2}$ tons = _____ lb.

### Compare. Write <, >, or =.

4. 96 oz. _____ 20 lb.      80 oz. _____ 6 lb.      3 lb. _____ 50 oz.

5. $1\frac{1}{2}$ tons _____ 3,000 lb.      320 oz. _____ 10 lb.      61 oz. _____ 4 lb.

6. 82 oz. _____ 5 lb.      6 tons _____ 10,000 lb.      100 oz. _____ 7 lb.

7. $\frac{1}{2}$ ton _____ 1,000 lbs.      32,000 oz. _____ 1 ton      1,600 oz. _____ 100 lb.

### Solve the problems.

8. Susan uses 30 inches of ribbon to make one bow. How many feet of ribbon are needed to make 10 bows?

9. At the end of a bike ride, everyone drank a 16 fluid ounce bottle of sports drink. If 12 kids and 2 adults were on the bike ride, how many quarts of sports drink did the riders drink?

10. How many pounds of nails will be needed to fill 100 boxes with 8 oz. of nails in each?

# Pre-Test: Multiplying and Dividing Whole Numbers

## Solve the equations.

1.
| 79 | 341 | 147 | 247 | 2,099 |
|---|---|---|---|---|
| x 7 | x 5 | x 2 | x 59 | x 6 |

2.
| 402 | 947 | 1,637 | 8,600 | 5,704 |
|---|---|---|---|---|
| x 88 | x 163 | x 22 | x 82 | x 822 |

## Divide. Write remainders where applicable.

3.     $7\overline{)63}$     $3\overline{)48}$     $6\overline{)546}$     $6\overline{)8{,}514}$

4.     $62\overline{)4{,}263}$     $32\overline{)6{,}744}$     $701\overline{)40{,}008}$     $165\overline{)67{,}042}$

## Solve the equations.

5.     $5 \times z = 45$     $x \div 8 = 64$     $k \times 6 = 216$     $y \div 5 = 125$

## Solve the problems.

6. Doug has been training all year to run in a marathon. He ran 63 miles each week for the past year (52 weeks). How many miles did Doug run altogether?

7. Kendra is knitting some blankets to sell at a craft fair. She has 215 feet of trim and she needs 23 feet for each blanket.

   How many blankets can she make?

   How much trim will she have left over?

29

# Multiplication

Multiply  6 x 783

<table>
<tr><td>

### Step 1
Multiply the ones.
Regroup.

6 x 3 = 18 ones, or
8 ones, 1 ten

</td><td>

### Step 2
Multiply the tens.
Regroup as needed.

(6 x 80) + 1 ten = 490, or
9 tens, 4 hundreds

</td><td>

### Step 3
Multiply the hundreds.

(6 x 700) + 4 hundreds =
4,600

</td></tr>
</table>

## Multiply.

**1.**

| 85 | 45 | 58 | 49 | 62 |
|---|---|---|---|---|
| x 5 | x 8 | x 2 | x 3 | x 7 |

**2.**

| 509 | 211 | 336 | 933 | 835 |
|---|---|---|---|---|
| x 9 | x 4 | x 5 | x 6 | x 3 |

**3.**

| 362 | 841 | 537 | 719 | 631 |
|---|---|---|---|---|
| x 8 | x 5 | x 3 | x 6 | x 9 |

**4.**

| 9,543 | 5,786 | 3,215 | 28,601 | 9,783 |
|---|---|---|---|---|
| x 8 | x 7 | x 9 | x 2 | x 4 |

**5.**

| 3,675 | 5,810 | 4,861 | 9,283 | 8,614 |
|---|---|---|---|---|
| x 6 | x 9 | x 5 | x 3 | x 7 |

**6.**

| 27,524 | 85,412 | 39,567 | 48,418 | 75,629 |
|---|---|---|---|---|
| x 5 | x 3 | x 6 | x 4 | x 8 |

# Multiplying by a 2-Digit Number

| Step 1 | Step 2 | Step 3 |
|---|---|---|
| Multiply the ones. Regroup. | Multiply the tens. Regroup as needed. | Add. |

Step 1
$$\begin{array}{r} {}^{1}\phantom{0} \\ 75 \\ \times\,5\,2 \\ \hline 150 \end{array}$$

$2 \times 75 = 150$

Step 2
$$\begin{array}{r} {}^{2}\phantom{0} \\ 75 \\ \times\,5\,2 \\ \hline 150 \\ 3{,}75\underline{0} \end{array}$$

Write a zero here if it helps.

$50 \times 75 = 3{,}750$

Step 3
$$\begin{array}{r} 75 \\ \times\,5\,2 \\ \hline 150 \\ +\,3750 \\ \hline 3900 \end{array}$$

## Multiply.

**1.**

| | | | | |
|---|---|---|---|---|
| 25 | 32 | 24 | 61 | 78 |
| x 74 | x 59 | x 96 | x 56 | x 14 |

**2.**

| | | | | |
|---|---|---|---|---|
| 48 | 86 | 62 | 78 | 95 |
| x 44 | x 57 | x 96 | x 36 | x 34 |

**3.**

| | | | | |
|---|---|---|---|---|
| 953 | 444 | 872 | 709 | 414 |
| x 25 | x 38 | x 19 | x 56 | x 41 |

**4.**

| | | | | |
|---|---|---|---|---|
| 779 | 982 | 486 | 695 | 728 |
| x 98 | x 63 | x 72 | x 89 | x 56 |

**5.**

| | | | | |
|---|---|---|---|---|
| 5,261 | 5,086 | 2,158 | 6,572 | 6,321 |
| x 39 | x 57 | x 73 | x 94 | x 62 |

**6.**

| | | | | |
|---|---|---|---|---|
| 9,831 | 2,156 | 4,127 | 3,333 | 4,066 |
| x 85 | x 39 | x 28 | x 76 | x 73 |

# Multiplying by a 3-Digit Number

Multiply **494 x 872**

| Step 1<br>Multiply by the ones digit. | Step 2<br>Multiply by the tens digit. | Step 3<br>Multiply by the hundreds digit. | Step 4<br>Add the partial products. |
|---|---|---|---|
| ²<br>8 7 2<br>x 4 9 4<br>**3, 4 8 8**<br><br>**4 x 872** | ⁶ ¹<br>8 7 2<br>x 4 9 4<br>3, 4 8 8<br>**7 8, 4 8 0**<br><br>**90 x 872** | ²<br>8 7 2<br>x 4 9 4<br>3, 4 8 8<br>7 8, 4 8 0<br>**3 4 8, 8 0 0**<br><br>**400 x 872** | 8 7 2<br>x 4 9 4<br>**3, 4 8 8**<br>**7 8, 4 8 0**<br>**+ 3 4 8, 8 0 0**<br>**4 3 0, 7 6 8** |

## Multiply.

**1.**

| 762 | 503 | 638 | 982 | 594 |
|---|---|---|---|---|
| x 381 | x 741 | x 897 | x 872 | x 439 |

**2.**

| 287 | 758 | 165 | 284 | 477 |
|---|---|---|---|---|
| x 287 | x 439 | x 825 | x 833 | x 360 |

**3.**

| 383 | 460 | 598 | 963 | 789 |
|---|---|---|---|---|
| x 103 | x 342 | x 636 | x 328 | x 951 |

**4.**

| 4,610 | 3,944 | 2,775 | 1,615 | 2,138 |
|---|---|---|---|---|
| x 239 | x 307 | x 173 | x 239 | x 256 |

**5.**

| 1,953 | 3,126 | 8,362 | 1,234 | 2,434 |
|---|---|---|---|---|
| x 279 | x 382 | x 123 | x 228 | x 327 |

**6.**

| 3,681 | 3,607 | 7,576 | 5,321 | 7,604 |
|---|---|---|---|---|
| x 453 | x 422 | x 531 | x 630 | x 126 |

Math Connection—Grade 6—RBP0180     www.summerbridgeactivities.com     © RBP Books

# Division: Dividing Whole Numbers by 1–Digit Divisors

Divide  3)1,585

**Step 1**
There are not enough thousands to divide. Decide where to place the first digit.

**Think:** 3)15

The first digit of the quotient will be in the hundreds place.

**Step 2**
Divide the hundreds.

```
    → 5
3)1585    Multiply 5 x 3
  −15      Subtract 15 −15
    0      Compare 0 < 3
```

**Step 3**
Bring down the 8 tens.

**Think:** 3)8

```
   52
3)1585
  −15
   08    Multiply 2 x 3
  − 6    Subtract 8 − 6
    2    Compare 2 < 3
```

**Step 4**
Bring down the 5 ones.

**Think:** 3)25

```
   528 R1
3)1585
  −15
   08
  − 6
   25    Multiply 8 x 3
  −24    Subtract 25 − 24
    1    Compare 1 < 3
```

Check your answer! Multiply the quotient by the divisor. Add the remainder to the product. The result should be the dividend.

```
  528      →   quotient
x   3      →   divisor
1,584      →   product
+   1      →   remainder
1,585      →   dividend
```

## Divide. Check your answers.

1.   3)643        4)857        6)674        5)569        3)605

2.   7)1,481      6)1,624      5)4,566      4)2,050      8)5,666

3.   8)2,495      7)4,985      4)2,601      2)1,734      6)2,532

www.summerbridgeactivities.com            **Math Connection—Grade 6—RBP0180**

# Division: Dividing Whole Numbers by 2-Digit Divisors

Divide **32**$\overline{)7{,}980}$

**Step 1**
There are not enough thousands to divide. Estimate to place the first digit in the quotient.

Use rounding to estimate.

**Think:** 30$\overline{)80}$
$80 \div 30$ is about 2

The first digit of the quotient will be in the hundreds place.

**Step 2**
Multiply. Subtract. Compare. Bring down the next digit.

```
        2
32 ) 7980      Multiply 2 x 32
    −64        Subtract 79 − 64
    158        Compare 15 < 32
               Bring down the 8.
```

The digits are really coming down today!

**Step 3**
Multiply. Subtract. Compare. Bring down the next digit.

```
       249 R12
32 ) 7980
    −64
    158        Multiply 4 x 32
   −128        Subtract 158 − 128
    300        Compare 30 < 32
   −288        Bring down the 0.
     12        (Repeat steps)
```
The remainder must always be less than the divisor.

## Divide. Check your answers.

1.  46$\overline{)857}$        28$\overline{)635}$        32$\overline{)8{,}329}$        55$\overline{)1{,}728}$

2.  21$\overline{)4{,}670}$        17$\overline{)4{,}287}$        58$\overline{)2{,}439}$        73$\overline{)8{,}967}$

3.  91$\overline{)8{,}743}$        52$\overline{)2{,}647}$        37$\overline{)86{,}322}$        48$\overline{)97{,}243}$

# Division: Dividing Whole Numbers by 3–Digit Divisors

Remember:
**D**ivide
**M**ultiply
**S**ubtract
**C**ompare
**B**ring Down

Dividing by 3-digit numbers is similar to dividing by 2-digit numbers.

**Example:** $397\overline{)23,925}$

Estimate to place the first digit in the quotient:

$$400\overline{)24,000}^{\quad 60}$$

$$\begin{array}{r} 60 \text{ R } 105 \\ 397\overline{)23,925} \\ -\,2,382 \\ \hline 105 \\ -\ \ 0 \\ \hline 105 \end{array}$$

## Divide. Check your answers.

1.  $845\overline{)5,070}$        $405\overline{)3,240}$        $624\overline{)4,368}$        $832\overline{)3,736}$

2.  $123\overline{)8,711}$        $537\overline{)3,765}$        $189\overline{)6,498}$        $273\overline{)74,618}$

3.  $213\overline{)65,827}$      $181\overline{)90,699}$      $289\overline{)79,346}$      $964\overline{)385,678}$

# Multiplication and Division Practice

## How's Business?

**Soldier:**          "Mine is

| 138,788 | 453 R2 | 1,944 | 98 R42 | |
|---|---|---|---|---|

| 5,844 | 103 R209 | 61,318 | 57,762 | |
|---|---|---|---|---|

| 98 R42 | 61 R4 | 61,318 | 1,484 | 1,944 |
|---|---|---|---|---|

**Steak House Chef:**    "Mine is

| 6 R52 | 104 R2 | 209,746 | 1,944 | 57,762 |
|---|---|---|---|---|

| 28,288 | 103 R209 | 1,944 | | |
|---|---|---|---|---|

| 4 R1 | 57,762 | 61 R4 | 209,746 | |
|---|---|---|---|---|

**Teacher:**          "Mine is

| 2,376 R9 | 10,080 | 61 R4 | 1,944 | 1,944 | 4 R1 |
|---|---|---|---|---|---|

Each person above is answering the question, "How's business?" To decode their answers, do the exercises below and find your answer in the code above. Each time the answer appears in the code, write the letter of that exercise above it. Keep working until you have decoded all three responses.

| **S** $243 \times 8$ | **D** $442 \times 64$ | **T** $5,432 \div 55$ |
|---|---|---|
| **O** $834 \div 8$ | **W** $496 \div 74$ | **N** $989 \times 62$ |
| **E** $9 \times 6,418$ | **J** $221 \times 628$ | **C** $42,777 \div 18$ |
| **Y** $289 \div 72$ | **U** $2,720 \div 6$ | **R** $527 \times 398$ |
| **K** $53 \times 28$ | **F** $487 \times 12$ | **I** $56,859 \div 550$ |
| **A** $2,566 \div 42$ | **L** $420 \times 24$ | |

Math Connection—Grade 6—RBP0180          www.summerbridgeactivities.com          © RBP Books

# Solving Multiplication Equations

To solve addition and subtraction equations, you use **inverse operations**. To solve multiplication equations, you also use inverse operations. The inverse of multiplying by a nonzero number is dividing by that number.

Solve:  $6 \cdot y = 54$

1. **Think:** What number times 6 is equal to 54?

2. Choose the inverse operation: Divide the other side of the equation by 6.

3. Simplify.

4. Check your solution: Substitute 9 for $y$ to see if the equation is true.

$y \cdot 6 = 54$

$y = 54 \div \mathbf{6}$

$y = 9$

$6 \cdot y = 54$

$6 \cdot 9 = 54$

$54 = 54$

| When working with equations, the $\cdot$ is often used as a symbol for "multiply." |

**Remember:** Division is the inverse of multiplication.

The equation is true, so the solution is correct.

## Complete the steps and solve the equations.

1.
$t \cdot 8 = 72$          $n \cdot 9 = 81$          $y \cdot 6 = 42$

$t = 72 \div \underline{\,8\,}$          $n = 81 \div \underline{\quad}$          $y = 42 \div \underline{\quad}$

$t = \underline{\,9\,}$          $n = \underline{\quad}$          $y = \underline{\quad}$

2.
$z \cdot 7 = 35$          $h \cdot 5 = 50$          $k \cdot 7 = 56$

$z = 35 \div \underline{\quad}$          $h = 50 \div \underline{\quad}$          $k = 56 \div \underline{\quad}$

$z = \underline{\quad}$          $h = \underline{\quad}$          $k = \underline{\quad}$

3.
$x \cdot 3 = 12$          $v \cdot 6 = 24$          $h \cdot 8 = 64$          $g \cdot 9 = 27$

4.
$n \cdot 6 = 48$          $j \cdot 7 = 14$          $t \cdot 5 = 25$          $d \cdot 4 = 40$

5.
$b \cdot 7 = 28$          $f \cdot 3 = 51$          $c \cdot 3 = 36$          $r \cdot 2 = 26$

## Solving Division Equations

Solve: $n/8 = 9$

1. **Think:** What number divided by 8 is equal to 9?
2. Choose the inverse operation: Multiply the other side of the equation by 8.
3. Simplify.
4. Check your solution: Substitute 72 for $n$ to see if the equation is true.

$n/8 = 9$

$n = 9 \cdot 8$

$n = 72$

$n \div 8 = 9$

$72 \div 8 = 9$

$9 = 9$

The fraction bar is also a division bar: $n/8$ is the same as $n \div 8$.

Multiplication is the inverse of division.

The equation is true, so the solution is correct.

## Complete the steps and solve the equations.

1. $x/9 = 4$          $f \div 8 = 7$          $y/4 = 16$

   $x = 4 \cdot \underline{9}$          $f = 7 \cdot \underline{\phantom{0}}$          $y = 16 \cdot \underline{\phantom{0}}$

   $x = \underline{36}$          $f = \underline{\phantom{0}}$          $y = \underline{\phantom{0}}$

2. $v \div 18 = 25$          $n/16 = 24$          $k \div 12 = 15$

   $v = 25 \cdot \underline{\phantom{0}}$          $n = 24 \cdot \underline{\phantom{0}}$          $k = 15 \cdot \underline{\phantom{0}}$

   $v = \underline{\phantom{0}}$          $n = \underline{\phantom{0}}$          $k = \underline{\phantom{0}}$

3. $b \div 7 = 7$          $p \div 6 = 4$          $t \div 9 = 7$          $j \div 7 = 6$

4. $c/5 = 10$          $g \div 4 = 9$          $y/25 = 75$          $s \div 22 = 11$

5. $w/9 = 102$          $k/30 = 18$          $d/82 = 6$          $z/29 = 16$

# Problem Solving Practice

A roller coaster ride at the American Eagle Amusement Park usually operates 4 trains, each of which carry 32 people. During the park's peak hours, 1,250 people wait in line to get on the roller coaster ride.

**1.** How many people can be on the ride at one time if all 4 cars are running?

**2.** How many times would each car have to run so that all 1,250 people could take the ride?

**3.** If the ride takes 4 minutes, including loading and unloading, about how long would it take for all 1,250 people in line to have a ride?

**4.** If the ride ran 5 cars instead of 4, how much less time would it take for all 1,250 people to have a ride?

**5.** The roller coaster structure is covered with 8,500 gallons of industrial white paint. How many quarts of paint is this?

**6.** About 15 tons of nails were used to build the roller coaster. About how many pounds of nails is this?

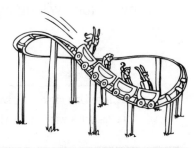

www.summerbridgeactivities.com    **Math Connection—Grade 6—RBP0180**

## Problem Solving Practice

1. The Perfectly Popped Popcorn Company did a study and found that the average popcorn consumer eats about 65 quarts of popcorn a year. If you eat this much, how many quarts of popcorn will you have consumed in 20 years?

   How many gallons will you have consumed in 20 years?

2. How long will it take you to consume 585 quarts of popcorn if you eat 65 quarts per year?

3. Perfectly Popped sells a variety of popcorn flavors in large, decorated tubs. If Jenna orders 36 matching tubs containing 216 gallons of popcorn in all, how much popcorn is in each tub?

4. The staff at a theater snack counter have found that 32 oz. of popcorn kernels makes enough popcorn to fill 20 small bags. How many small bags could they fill with 18 pounds of popcorn?

5. The cargo trucks that distribute the packaged popcorn to retailers hold 95 tubs of popcorn each. How many trucks will it take to distribute 1,250 tubs of popcorn?

   If each truck is filled to capacity, how many tubs will be on the last truck?

   **Clue:** Use logical reasoning. One truck will not be filled to capacity.

6. Perfectly Popped received a shipment of 227 boxes of popcorn kernels. These were divided into 8 groups. Each group contained 28 boxes except one. How many boxes were in that group?

   **Clue:** You will need to interpret the remainder.

# Post-Test: Multiplying and Dividing Whole Numbers

**Multiply.**

1.
$$\begin{array}{r} 37 \\ \times\ 4 \end{array}$$
$$\begin{array}{r} 415 \\ \times\ 6 \end{array}$$
$$\begin{array}{r} 542 \\ \times\ 81 \end{array}$$
$$\begin{array}{r} 427 \\ \times\ 22 \end{array}$$

2.
$$\begin{array}{r} 4{,}804 \\ \times\ 7 \end{array}$$
$$\begin{array}{r} 647 \\ \times\ 142 \end{array}$$
$$\begin{array}{r} 6{,}521 \\ \times\ 34 \end{array}$$
$$\begin{array}{r} 1{,}254 \\ \times\ 89 \end{array}$$

**Divide.**

3.  $9\overline{)81}$      $9\overline{)828}$      $4\overline{)39}$      $8\overline{)965}$

4.  $5\overline{)4{,}517}$      $17\overline{)60}$      $17\overline{)5{,}209}$      $189\overline{)16{,}350}$

**Solve the equations.**

5.  $z \cdot 12 = 60$      $x \div 10 = 12$      $9 \cdot k = 153$      $y/17 = 43$

**Solve each problem.**

6. Susan owns a chain of dress shops. Last month she sold 1,432 dresses. Each dress sold for an average of $65. How much money did Susan make on the dresses?

7. Mitchell has collected 1,327 marbles. He has divided the marbles equally into 12 jars. How many marbles are in each jar?

How many marbles are left over?

# Metric Measurement

The basic unit for measuring length in the metric system is the **meter**.

| Divide | Multiply |
|---|---|
| To change from a lesser unit to a greater unit. | To change from a greater unit to a lesser unit. |

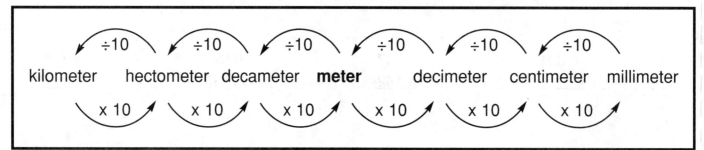

kilometer    hectometer   decameter   **meter**    decimeter   centimeter   millimeter

**Example:** Use a ruler to measure this line segment to the nearest centimeter and millimeter.

This length is closer to 6 cm than 7 cm, so to the nearest centimeter the length is 6 cm.
To the nearest millimeter, the line segment measures 63 mm.

## Use a ruler to measure each line segment to the nearest centimeter and millimeter.

1. _____

2. _____

3. _____

4. _____

5. _____

## Convert these measurements.

6.     7 m = _____ cm            6 m = _____ dm            3,500 cm = _____ m

7.     82 dm = _____ cm         8 km = _____ m           19,000 m = _____ km

Math Connection—Grade 6—RBP0180       www.summerbridgeactivities.com       ©RBP Books

# Pre-Test: Fractions

1. Write each missing fraction on the number line below.

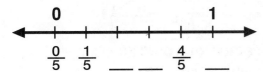

0           1

$\frac{0}{5}$   $\frac{1}{5}$   ___   ___   $\frac{4}{5}$   ___

Hey! There's only a fraction of this pie left!

2. Circle all the fractions that are equal to $\frac{9}{12}$.

$\frac{12}{16}$     $\frac{3}{4}$     $\frac{2}{3}$     $\frac{21}{28}$     $\frac{30}{40}$     $\frac{24}{36}$

## Find the greatest common factor (GCF) for each pair of numbers.

3.    44, 33          28, 35          48, 36          20, 50

## Write each fraction in simplest form.

4.      $\frac{6}{9}$ = ___            $\frac{18}{60}$ = ___            $\frac{12}{54}$ = ___

## Find the least common multiple (LCM) for each pair of numbers.

5.    10, 20          18, 36          12, 18          3, 5

## Find the least common multiple (LCM) for each pair of fractions.

6.      $\frac{1}{4}$ and $\frac{4}{8}$         $\frac{2}{3}$ and $\frac{4}{5}$         $\frac{3}{12}$ and $\frac{6}{8}$

7.      $\frac{2}{3}$ and $\frac{6}{9}$         $\frac{2}{5}$ and $\frac{3}{4}$         $\frac{4}{10}$ and $\frac{6}{15}$

## Compare. Write >, <, or = .

8.      $\frac{2}{3}$ ___ $\frac{3}{5}$         $\frac{5}{12}$ ___ $\frac{1}{3}$         $\frac{7}{10}$ ___ $\frac{5}{9}$

## Solve.

9. Kevin answered 40 out of 48 questions correctly on a test he took at school. What is the fraction of answers he got correct, written in simplest form?

# Fractions: Write Fractions

You can represent fractions on a number line. If an interval of length 1 is divided into 6 equal pieces, the length of any one of the pieces represents $\frac{1}{6}$.

The fraction $\frac{1}{6}$ can also be thought of as $1 \div 6$ since the interval is divided into 6 equal parts.

**Remember:**

$\frac{5}{6} = \frac{\text{numerator}}{\text{denominator}}$

The **numerator** is the number of parts or groups represented.

The **denominator** is the total number of parts or groups.

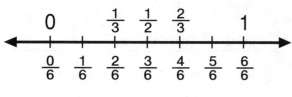

## Write each missing fraction on the number lines.

The first one has been done for you.

**1.**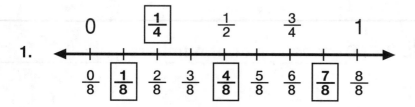

**2.**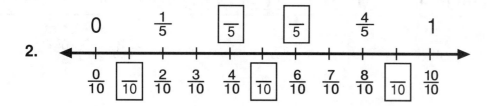

**3.**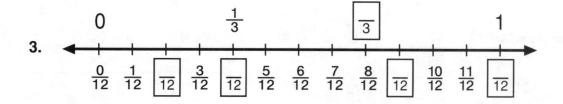

**4.**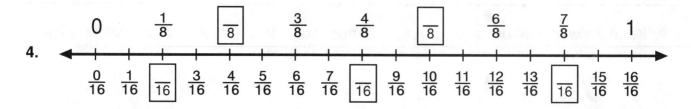

**Math Connection—Grade 6—RBP0180**         www.summerbridgeactivities.com     ©RBP Books

# Fractions: Equivalent Fractions

**Example:**  $\dfrac{4}{6} = \dfrac{4 \times 2}{6 \times 2} = \dfrac{8}{12}$

$\dfrac{4}{6} = \dfrac{4 \times 3}{6 \times 3} = \dfrac{12}{18}$

$\dfrac{4}{6} = \dfrac{4 \div 2}{6 \div 2} = \dfrac{2}{3}$

So, $\dfrac{4}{6}$, $\dfrac{8}{12}$, $\dfrac{12}{18}$, and $\dfrac{2}{3}$ are all equivalent fractions.

**Equivalent Fraction Rule:**
If a numerator and a denominator are each multiplied or divided by the same number, then the new fraction represents the same number.

## For each fraction, write two equivalent fractions.

1.  $\dfrac{2}{4}$ $\qquad\qquad$ $\dfrac{2}{12}$ $\qquad\qquad$ $\dfrac{8}{14}$ $\qquad\qquad$ $\dfrac{4}{18}$

2.  $\dfrac{10}{24}$ $\qquad\qquad$ $\dfrac{4}{9}$ $\qquad\qquad$ $\dfrac{10}{20}$ $\qquad\qquad$ $\dfrac{18}{24}$

3.  $\dfrac{2}{16}$ $\qquad\qquad$ $\dfrac{10}{12}$ $\qquad\qquad$ $\dfrac{8}{9}$ $\qquad\qquad$ $\dfrac{4}{10}$

4.  $\dfrac{3}{24}$ $\qquad\qquad$ $\dfrac{3}{10}$ $\qquad\qquad$ $\dfrac{7}{18}$ $\qquad\qquad$ $\dfrac{18}{40}$

## Write an equivalent fraction.

5.  $\dfrac{1}{11} = \dfrac{}{33}$ $\qquad\qquad$ $\dfrac{1}{20} = \dfrac{4}{}$ $\qquad\qquad$ $\dfrac{4}{16} = \dfrac{}{32}$

6.  $\dfrac{3}{15} = \dfrac{}{45}$ $\qquad\qquad$ $\dfrac{12}{20} = \dfrac{36}{}$ $\qquad\qquad$ $\dfrac{5}{16} = \dfrac{}{48}$

7.  $\dfrac{3}{18} = \dfrac{}{36}$ $\qquad\qquad$ $\dfrac{12}{18} = \dfrac{}{54}$ $\qquad\qquad$ $\dfrac{1}{30} = \dfrac{3}{}$

8.  $\dfrac{7}{11} = \dfrac{42}{}$ $\qquad\qquad$ $\dfrac{4}{10} = \dfrac{}{50}$ $\qquad\qquad$ $\dfrac{10}{40} = \dfrac{30}{}$

www.summerbridgeactivities.com     Math Connection—Grade 6—RBP0180

# Fractions: Greatest Common Factor

**Example:** List the factors of 12 and 18. Circle the common factors. Write the greatest common factor (GCF).

Factors of 12: ①②③ 4, ⑥ 12

Factors of 18: ①②③⑥ 9, 18

Common Factors: ①②③⑥

**GCF=6**

A **factor** is a number that another number can be divided by evenly.

## List the factors of each pair of numbers. Circle the common factors. Find the greatest common factor (GCF).

1.    6:                              4:

      18:                          12:

      GCF_____                GCF_____

2.    12:                           14:

      18:                          21:

      GCF_____                GCF_____

3.    18:                           24:

      27:                          32:

      GCF_____                GCF_____

4.    9:                               9:

      12:                          15:

      GCF_____                GCF_____

5.    15:                           15:

      20:                          40:

      GCF_____                GCF_____

6.    14:                           15:

      35:                          35:

      GCF_____                GCF_____

Math Connection—Grade 6—RBP0180         www.summerbridgeactivities.com       ©RBP Books

# Fractions: Simplest Form

**Example:** Write the fraction $\frac{42}{56}$ in simplest form.

### Step 1
Find the GCF of the numerator and denominator.

42: ①②3, 6,⑦⑭㉑,㊷
56: ①②4,⑦8, ⑭ 28, 56

**GCF = 14**

### Step 2
Divide the numerator and denominator by their GCF.

$$\frac{42}{56} \div \frac{14}{14} = \frac{3}{4}$$

## Write each fraction in simplest form. Circle your answer.

If a fraction is already in simplest form, just write the fraction.

| | | | | | |
|---|---|---|---|---|---|
| **1.** | $\frac{4}{6}$ | $\frac{5}{10}$ | $\frac{9}{15}$ | $\frac{8}{14}$ | $\frac{2}{15}$ |
| **2.** | $\frac{3}{27}$ | $\frac{5}{18}$ | $\frac{15}{18}$ | $\frac{28}{30}$ | $\frac{5}{20}$ |
| **3.** | $\frac{6}{21}$ | $\frac{28}{42}$ | $\frac{22}{30}$ | $\frac{15}{32}$ | $\frac{35}{50}$ |
| **4.** | $\frac{7}{21}$ | $\frac{19}{38}$ | $\frac{48}{60}$ | $\frac{10}{20}$ | $\frac{22}{32}$ |
| **5.** | $\frac{34}{59}$ | $\frac{22}{88}$ | $\frac{26}{28}$ | $\frac{18}{90}$ | $\frac{75}{80}$ |
| **6.** | $\frac{30}{50}$ | $\frac{20}{100}$ | $\frac{25}{75}$ | $\frac{60}{200}$ | $\frac{4}{30}$ |

# Fractions: Least Common Multiple

The least common multiple (LCM) is the smallest number that is a multiple of two or more numbers.

**Example:** Find the LCM of 6 and 8.
- List some multiples of 6 and 8.
- Circle the common multiples.
- Write the least common multiple (LCM).

Multiples of 6:  6, 12, 18, (24) 30, 36, 42, (48)
Multiples of 8:  8, 16, (24) 32, 40, (48)

**LCM = 24**

## Find the least common multiple (LCM) of each pair of numbers.

1.    6:                           4:
           2:                           8:
           LCM_____           LCM_____

We have less in common...

...than these fractions!

2.    5:                           4:
           3:                           6:
           LCM_____           LCM_____

3.    8:                           6:
          12:                         10:
           LCM_____           LCM_____

4.   12:                         10:
          20:                         15:
           LCM_____           LCM_____

## Find the least common multiple (LCM) of each set of numbers.

5.    6:                           4:
           5:                           9:
         15:                         18:
           LCM_____           LCM_____

6.    8:                           10:
         10:                         15:
         20:                         30:
           LCM_____           LCM_____

       www.summerbridgeactivities.com        ©RBP Books

# Fractions: Lowest Common Denominator

Two fractions have a common denominator if their denominators are the same.

The **least common denominator** (**LCD**) of two fractions is the least common multiple of their denominators.

$\frac{5}{8}$ and $\frac{7}{12}$

**Step 1**
Find the LCD of the numerator and denominator.

8: 8, 16, 24
12: 12, 24

**LCD = 24**

**Step 2**
Write equivalent fractions with the common denominator of 24.

$\frac{5}{8} = \frac{\phantom{15}}{24}$
$\frac{5}{8} = \frac{5}{8} \times \frac{3}{3} = \frac{15}{24}$

$\frac{7}{12} = \frac{\phantom{14}}{24}$
$\frac{7}{12} = \frac{7}{12} \times \frac{2}{2} = \frac{14}{24}$

## Write equivalent fractions with the LCD.

1. $\frac{1}{9}$ and $\frac{1}{3}$     $\frac{1}{3}$ and $\frac{1}{6}$     $\frac{5}{6}$ and $\frac{2}{5}$

2. $\frac{4}{8}$ and $\frac{2}{3}$     $\frac{2}{6}$ and $\frac{3}{9}$     $\frac{4}{5}$ and $\frac{3}{9}$

3. $\frac{2}{4}$ and $\frac{3}{7}$     $\frac{2}{3}$ and $\frac{6}{8}$     $\frac{3}{5}$ and $\frac{5}{6}$

4. $\frac{1}{8}$ and $\frac{1}{16}$     $\frac{1}{12}$ and $\frac{1}{4}$     $\frac{1}{18}$ and $\frac{1}{9}$

5. $\frac{6}{9}$ and $\frac{3}{18}$     $\frac{2}{8}$ and $\frac{4}{32}$     $\frac{4}{5}$ and $\frac{6}{20}$

6. $\frac{1}{4}$ and $\frac{3}{18}$     $\frac{3}{7}$ and $\frac{3}{8}$     $\frac{1}{2}$ and $\frac{4}{11}$

# Fractions: Comparing and Ordering

To compare fractions, you need common denominators.

**Example:** Compare $\frac{5}{7}$ and $\frac{7}{9}$.

**Step 1**
Find the LCD.

7: 7, 14, 21, 28, 35, 42, 49, 56, **63**
9: 9, 18, 27, 36, 45, 54, **63**

**LCD = 63**

**Step 2**
Write equivalent fractions with the LCD.

$\frac{5}{7} = \frac{}{63}$

$\frac{5}{7} = \frac{5}{7} \times \frac{9}{9} = \frac{45}{63}$

$\frac{7}{9} = \frac{}{63}$

$\frac{7}{9} = \frac{7}{9} \times \frac{7}{7} = \frac{49}{63}$

**Step 3**
Compare the numerators.

$\frac{45}{63} < \frac{49}{63}$

## Compare. Write >, <, or = in the ◯ in each problem.

1.  $\frac{3}{6} \bigcirc \frac{4}{8}$     $\frac{4}{5} \bigcirc \frac{10}{15}$     $\frac{3}{5} \bigcirc \frac{1}{2}$     $\frac{2}{7} \bigcirc \frac{1}{3}$

2.  $\frac{2}{3} \bigcirc \frac{5}{8}$     $\frac{1}{3} \bigcirc \frac{2}{5}$     $\frac{1}{8} \bigcirc \frac{1}{16}$     $\frac{5}{9} \bigcirc \frac{4}{8}$

3.  $\frac{3}{5} \bigcirc \frac{2}{3}$     $\frac{7}{10} \bigcirc \frac{2}{3}$     $\frac{5}{8} \bigcirc \frac{10}{16}$     $\frac{2}{9} \bigcirc \frac{1}{3}$

## Order from least to greatest.

4.     $\frac{1}{3}, \frac{7}{12}, \frac{5}{6}$          $\frac{3}{4}, \frac{7}{8}, \frac{13}{16}$          $\frac{3}{4}, \frac{5}{7}, \frac{9}{14}$

5.     $\frac{5}{6}, \frac{3}{4}, \frac{1}{2}$          $\frac{3}{7}, \frac{3}{5}, \frac{3}{8}$          $\frac{4}{5}, \frac{17}{20}, \frac{3}{4}$

Math Connection—Grade 6—RBP0180                     www.summerbridgeactivities.com                     ©RBP Books

# Problem Solving

## Solve each problem. Write answers in simplest terms.

1. The picture to the right shows how much pizza is left. Write a fraction in simplest terms to show how much pizza was eaten.

2. An extra-large pepperoni pizza was cut into 16 equal slices. A total of 10 slices of pizza were eaten. What fraction of the pizza was left over?

3. The school cafeteria orders pizza every Friday from a local pizza factory. About $\frac{2}{3}$ of the students who eat the pizza for lunch prefer pepperoni. If the school orders 48 pizzas altogether, how many of these should be pepperoni?

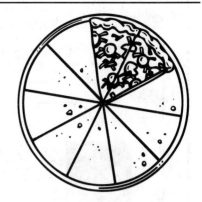

**Clue:**
Find a fraction equivalent to $\frac{2}{3}$.

4. Four friends shared a pizza. Maria ate $\frac{1}{3}$ of the pizza, Ally and Mindy each ate $\frac{1}{4}$ of the pizza, and Bethany ate $\frac{1}{6}$.

   **a.** Into how many equal slices did they need to cut the pizza?

   **b.** How many slices of pizza did each girl eat?

**Clue:**
Find equal fractions using the LCD.

5. In a survey on vegetable toppings, $\frac{3}{4}$ of the sixth-grade students said they liked green peppers on their pizza, $\frac{5}{8}$ said they liked mushrooms, and $\frac{2}{3}$ of the students said they liked onions. (Some students liked more than one choice.)

   **a.** Which of the three choices do more of the students like?

   **b.** Which of the three choices do the least number of students like?

**Clue:**
Order the fractions from greatest to least.

6. Each medium pizza weighs 54 ounces. The pizza dough alone weighs 21 ounces. What fraction of the pizza's weight is the pizza dough?

www.summerbridgeactivities.com **Math Connection—Grade 6—RBP0180**

# Problem Solving: Using Fractions in a Bar Graph

The Chamber of Commerce surveyed tourists to see what activities they participated in while visiting the capital city. The graph shows the fraction of all tourists who took part in each activity.

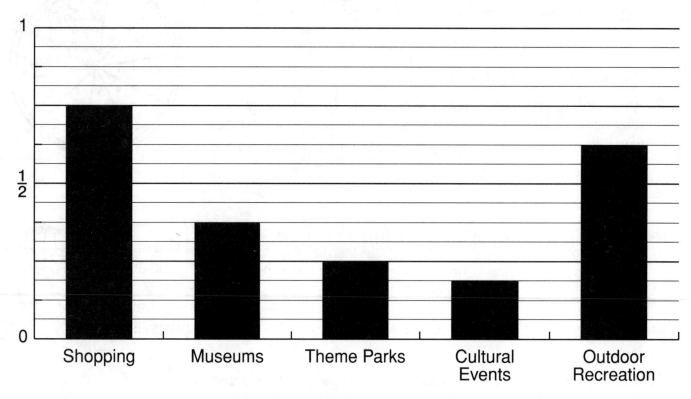

## Solve using the graph. Write all fractions in simplest form.

1. Which activities were chosen by more than $\frac{1}{2}$ of the tourists?

2. What fraction of tourists participated in the least popular activity?

3. What fraction of the tourists participated in the most popular activity?

4. Which activity did $\frac{5}{8}$ of the tourists participate in?

5. What fraction of the tourists visited theme parks?

6. Which activity was participated in half as much as shopping?

**Think:**
What denominator should you use to compare the data?

7. Which activity did $\frac{1}{4}$ of the tourists participate in?

www.summerbridgeactivities.com

## Post-Test: Fractions

1. Write each missing fraction on the number line below.

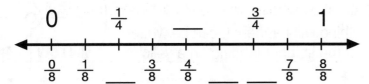

$$0 \qquad \frac{1}{4} \qquad \underline{\qquad} \qquad \frac{3}{4} \qquad 1$$

$$\frac{0}{8} \quad \frac{1}{8} \quad \underline{\qquad} \quad \frac{3}{8} \quad \frac{4}{8} \quad \underline{\qquad} \quad \underline{\qquad} \quad \frac{7}{8} \quad \frac{8}{8}$$

2. Circle all the fractions that are equal to $\frac{6}{16}$.

$$\frac{3}{8} \qquad \frac{1}{3} \qquad \frac{9}{24} \qquad \frac{6}{24} \qquad \frac{12}{32} \qquad \frac{18}{36}$$

## Find the greatest common factor (GCF) for each pair of numbers.

3.      40, 15            15, 35            12, 30            40, 60

## Write each fraction in simplest form.

4.      $\frac{6}{8} = \underline{\qquad}$            $\frac{14}{16} = \underline{\qquad}$            $\frac{25}{75} = \underline{\qquad}$

## Find the least common multiple (LCM) for each pair of numbers.

5.      20, 30            12, 20            4, 14            5, 7

## Write equivalent fractions with the lowest common denominator (LCD).

6.      $\frac{1}{3}$ and $\frac{7}{9}$            $\frac{3}{5}$ and $\frac{2}{4}$            $\frac{4}{10}$ and $\frac{3}{4}$

7.      $\frac{3}{8}$ and $\frac{1}{2}$            $\frac{2}{3}$ and $\frac{4}{5}$            $\frac{6}{10}$ and $\frac{8}{15}$

## Compare. Write >, <, or = .

8.      $\frac{3}{4} \underline{\qquad} \frac{7}{10}$            $\frac{6}{8} \underline{\qquad} \frac{7}{9}$            $\frac{11}{15} \underline{\qquad} \frac{21}{30}$

## Solve.

9. Shelly made 36 cookies; 21 were chocolate chip. Written in simplest form, what is the fraction of chocolate chip cookies she made?

# Probability

What is the probability that the spinner will land on yellow?

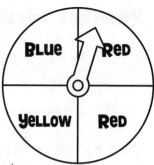

**Probability** tells how likely it is that something will happen. It can be written as a fraction. To determine the probability of the spinner landing on a yellow space, do the following:

$$P \text{ (yellow)} = \frac{\text{Number of Yellow Spaces}}{\text{Number of Spaces Possible}} = \frac{1}{4} \quad \frac{\textbf{Favorable Outcomes (chance)}}{\textbf{Possible Outcomes (possibilities)}}$$

The probability that the spinner will land on yellow is $\frac{1}{4}$.

For red, $P \text{ (red)} = \dfrac{\text{Number of Red Spaces}}{\text{Number of Spaces Possible}} = \dfrac{2}{4} = \dfrac{1}{2}$.

The probability that the spinner will land on red is $\frac{1}{2}$.

---

A jar contains 18 marbles that are all the same size. It contains 7 purple, 3 green, and 8 orange marbles. Without looking, Travis picks one marble. What is the probability of each of the following outcomes? The first one has been done for you.

1.  $P \text{ (green)} = \frac{3}{18} = \frac{1}{6}$      $P \text{ (purple)} =$      $P \text{ (orange)} =$

2.  $P \text{ (not green)} =$      $P \text{ (purple or green)} =$      $P \text{ (not orange)} =$

3.  $P \text{ (not purple)} =$      $P \text{ (orange or green)} =$      $P \text{ (purple, green, or orange)} =$

Of 16 socks in Jenn's drawer, 6 are brown, 4 are black, 2 are gray, and 4 are blue. Find the probability of each.

4.  $P \text{ (not brown)} = \frac{10}{16} = \frac{5}{8}$      $P \text{ (gray)} =$      $P \text{ (blue)} =$

5.  $P \text{ (blue or black)} =$      $P \text{ (not black)} =$      $P \text{ (blue, gray, or black)} =$

A 6-sided number cube numbered 1 through 6 is randomly tossed. Find the probability of tossing each outcome.

6.  $P \text{ (5)} =$      $P \text{ (1 or 2)} =$      $P \text{ (odd number)} =$

7.  $P \text{ (not 6)} =$      $P \text{ (even number)} =$      $P \text{ (1, 2, 3, or 4)} =$

# Pre-Test: Adding and Subtracting Fractions

**Write an improper fraction for each mixed number.**

1.    $2\frac{1}{3}$              $4\frac{3}{8}$              $6\frac{3}{5}$              $11\frac{5}{6}$

**Write a mixed number for each improper fraction.**

2.    $\frac{23}{7}$              $\frac{52}{8}$              $\frac{14}{2}$              $\frac{85}{16}$

**Add or subtract. Write all answers in simplest form.**

3.    $\begin{array}{r}\frac{1}{5}\\[4pt]+\ \frac{3}{5}\\\hline\end{array}$              $\begin{array}{r}\frac{3}{8}\\[4pt]+\ \frac{7}{8}\\\hline\end{array}$              $\begin{array}{r}\frac{2}{3}\\[4pt]+\ \frac{2}{5}\\\hline\end{array}$              $\begin{array}{r}\frac{7}{18}\\[4pt]+\ \frac{12}{36}\\\hline\end{array}$

4.    $\begin{array}{r}\frac{5}{6}\\[4pt]-\ \frac{1}{6}\\\hline\end{array}$              $\begin{array}{r}\frac{5}{6}\\[4pt]-\ \frac{1}{4}\\\hline\end{array}$              $\begin{array}{r}\frac{11}{12}\\[4pt]-\ \frac{4}{5}\\\hline\end{array}$              $\begin{array}{r}\frac{2}{3}\\[4pt]-\ \frac{5}{9}\\\hline\end{array}$

5.    $\begin{array}{r}9\frac{2}{3}\\[4pt]+\ 1\frac{1}{3}\\\hline\end{array}$              $\begin{array}{r}2\frac{1}{2}\\[4pt]+\ 2\frac{3}{5}\\\hline\end{array}$              $\begin{array}{r}7\frac{5}{8}\\[4pt]+\ 6\frac{3}{4}\\\hline\end{array}$              $\begin{array}{r}10\frac{3}{4}\\[4pt]+\ 5\frac{7}{10}\\\hline\end{array}$

6.    $\begin{array}{r}5\frac{7}{8}\\[4pt]-\ 3\frac{1}{8}\\\hline\end{array}$              $\begin{array}{r}6\frac{2}{3}\\[4pt]-\ 1\frac{4}{9}\\\hline\end{array}$              $\begin{array}{r}8\frac{1}{4}\\[4pt]-\ 3\frac{5}{6}\\\hline\end{array}$              $\begin{array}{r}9\frac{5}{6}\\[4pt]-\ 4\frac{5}{7}\\\hline\end{array}$

**Solve each problem. Write all answers in simplest form.**

7. Robert recorded a $2\frac{1}{2}$ hour movie and a $1\frac{3}{4}$ hour movie on one video tape. How many hours of movies are on the tapes?

8. The rainfall in Jane's town totaled $6\frac{1}{4}$ inches in April and $4\frac{1}{16}$ inches in May. How much more rain fell in April?

# Fractions: Writing Mixed Numbers

A **mixed number** is made up of a whole number and a fraction. A mixed number is a number greater than 1 that is between two whole numbers.

whole number → $3\frac{1}{2}$ ← fraction

$3\frac{1}{2}$ is the same as $3 + \frac{1}{2}$

An **improper fraction** has a numerator that is greater than or equal to the denominator. An improper fraction is greater than or equal to 1.

Improper fraction → $\frac{7}{2} = 3\frac{1}{2}$ ← mixed number

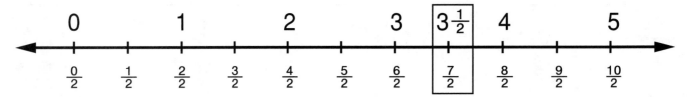

## Example:

Write $\frac{10}{4}$ as a mixed number.

The fraction bar stands for "divided by." So, $\frac{10}{4}$ means "10 divided by 4."

**Think:** How many times does 4 go into 10?
Four goes into ten **2 times, with 2 remaining**.
So, $\frac{10}{4} = 2\frac{2}{4} = 2\frac{1}{2}$

$$\begin{array}{r} 2 \leftarrow \text{number of wholes} \\ 4\overline{)10} \\ \underline{-8} \\ 2 \leftarrow \text{number of fourths remaining} \end{array}$$

## Write each fraction as a whole number or a mixed number.

1.　　$\frac{4}{3}$　　　　$\frac{5}{2}$　　　　$\frac{25}{5}$　　　　$\frac{17}{12}$　　　　$\frac{26}{3}$

2.　　$\frac{10}{3}$　　　　$\frac{81}{9}$　　　　$\frac{43}{13}$　　　　$\frac{31}{5}$　　　　$\frac{80}{12}$

3.　　$\frac{28}{3}$　　　　$\frac{51}{8}$　　　　$\frac{60}{9}$　　　　$\frac{60}{12}$　　　　$\frac{53}{8}$

4.　　$\frac{55}{11}$　　　　$\frac{17}{2}$　　　　$\frac{76}{10}$　　　　$\frac{27}{5}$　　　　$\frac{11}{3}$

Math Connection—Grade 6—RBP0180          www.summerbridgeactivities.com          ©RBP Books

# Fractions: Writing Improper Fractions

Write $5\frac{2}{5}$ as an improper fraction.     Think: $5\frac{2}{5} = 5 + \frac{2}{5} = \frac{25}{5} + \frac{2}{5} = \frac{27}{5}$

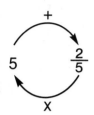

$5 \times 5 = 25$

$25 + 2 = 27$

$5\frac{2}{5} = \frac{27}{5}$

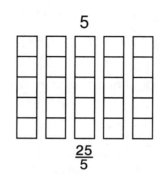

$5$      $+$     $\frac{2}{5}$    $=$    $5\frac{2}{5}$

$\frac{25}{5}$      $+$     $\frac{2}{5}$    $=$    $\frac{27}{5}$

Rename 3 as a fraction with a denominator of 5.

$3 = \overline{\phantom{0}5}$

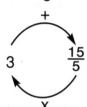

Multiply the 3
and the 5 to find
the numerator.

My goodness,
these fractions
are improper!

## Write each mixed number as an improper fraction.

1.    $8\frac{2}{3}$        $5\frac{2}{5}$        $2\frac{9}{18}$        $4\frac{3}{8}$

2.    $6\frac{3}{4}$        $3\frac{3}{7}$        $10\frac{2}{3}$        $12\frac{3}{4}$

3.    $10\frac{2}{5}$        $11\frac{1}{11}$        $1\frac{7}{16}$        $8\frac{8}{12}$

4.    $6\frac{10}{12}$        $3\frac{10}{16}$        $5\frac{1}{16}$        $12\frac{7}{12}$

## Write each whole number as a fraction.

5.    $1 = \overline{\phantom{0}5}$        $1 = \overline{\phantom{0}12}$        $4 = \overline{\phantom{0}2}$        $6 = \overline{\phantom{0}4}$

6.    $8 = \overline{\phantom{0}3}$        $10 = \overline{\phantom{0}3}$        $12 = \overline{\phantom{0}5}$        $16 = \overline{\phantom{0}2}$

7.    $18 = \overline{\phantom{0}3}$        $11 = \overline{\phantom{0}5}$        $13 = \overline{\phantom{0}2}$        $15 = \overline{\phantom{0}5}$

# Fractions: Adding and Subtracting Like Denominators

To add or subtract fractions that have the same denominator:

**Step 1**
Add or subtract the numerators to find the numerator of the answer.

$$\frac{1}{8} + \frac{3}{8} = \frac{4}{\quad}$$

**Step 2**
Write the denominator of the fractions as the denominator of the answer.

$$\frac{1}{8} + \frac{3}{8} = \frac{4}{8}$$

**Step 3**
Write the sum or difference in simplest form.

$$\frac{4}{8} = \frac{1}{2}$$

$$\frac{1}{8} + \frac{3}{8} = \frac{4}{8} \text{ or } \frac{1}{2}$$

$$\frac{7}{8} - \frac{3}{8} = \frac{4}{8} \text{ or } \frac{1}{2}$$

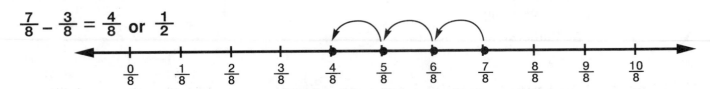

## Write each sum or difference in simplest form.

1. $\dfrac{5}{7} - \dfrac{4}{7} =$    $\dfrac{3}{10} + \dfrac{7}{10} =$    $\dfrac{7}{12} - \dfrac{1}{12} =$

2. $\dfrac{5}{6} + \dfrac{5}{6} =$    $\dfrac{2}{15} + \dfrac{8}{15} =$    $\dfrac{2}{5} + \dfrac{4}{5} =$

3. $\dfrac{15}{20} - \dfrac{8}{20} =$    $\dfrac{10}{11} - \dfrac{4}{11} =$    $\dfrac{9}{10} - \dfrac{4}{10} =$

4. $\begin{array}{r}\frac{4}{9} \\ +\frac{8}{9} \\ \hline\end{array}$    $\begin{array}{r}\frac{3}{5} \\ +\frac{4}{5} \\ \hline\end{array}$    $\begin{array}{r}\frac{5}{6} \\ -\frac{1}{6} \\ \hline\end{array}$    $\begin{array}{r}\frac{4}{9} \\ -\frac{2}{9} \\ \hline\end{array}$    $\begin{array}{r}\frac{2}{3} \\ -\frac{1}{3} \\ \hline\end{array}$

5. $\begin{array}{r}\frac{9}{10} \\ -\frac{3}{10} \\ \hline\end{array}$    $\begin{array}{r}\frac{4}{7} \\ +\frac{6}{7} \\ \hline\end{array}$    $\begin{array}{r}\frac{3}{8} \\ -\frac{1}{8} \\ \hline\end{array}$    $\begin{array}{r}\frac{5}{12} \\ +\frac{11}{12} \\ \hline\end{array}$    $\begin{array}{r}\frac{3}{4} \\ -\frac{1}{4} \\ \hline\end{array}$

# Fractions: Adding and Subtracting Mixed Numbers

To add or subtract mixed numbers whose fractions have the same denominator:

**Step 1**
Add or subtract the numerators of the fraction part.

$$2\frac{7}{9}$$
$$+\ 4\frac{8}{9}$$
$$\overline{\quad\frac{15}{9}}$$

**Step 2**
Add or subtract the whole numbers.

$$2\frac{7}{9}$$
$$+\ 4\frac{8}{9}$$
$$\overline{6\ \frac{15}{9}}$$

**Step 3**
Simplify.

$$2\frac{7}{9}$$
$$+\ 4\frac{8}{9}$$
$$\overline{6\frac{15}{9}}\ =$$
$$7\frac{6}{9}\ \text{or}\ 7\frac{2}{3}$$

## Write each sum or difference in simplest form.

**1.**
$3\frac{1}{3}$
$+\ 1\frac{2}{3}$

$6\frac{7}{10}$
$-\ 2\frac{3}{10}$

$4\frac{5}{6}$
$-\ \frac{1}{6}$

$4\frac{7}{8}$
$+\ 1\frac{1}{8}$

$2\frac{4}{9}$
$-\ 1\frac{1}{9}$

**2.**
$4\frac{1}{2}$
$+\ 4\frac{1}{2}$

$5\frac{2}{3}$
$-\ 4$

$3\frac{1}{2}$
$-\ 1\frac{1}{2}$

$3\frac{7}{12}$
$-\ 2\frac{1}{12}$

$6\frac{4}{5}$
$+\ 3\frac{3}{5}$

**3.**
$7\frac{3}{8}$
$-\ 5$

$6\frac{3}{4}$
$+\ \frac{3}{4}$

$5\frac{11}{14}$
$-\ 2\frac{3}{14}$

$8\frac{3}{15}$
$+\ 7\frac{7}{15}$

$4\frac{6}{7}$
$-\ 1\frac{2}{7}$

**4.**
$3\frac{5}{12}$
$-\ 2$

$7\frac{2}{3}$
$-\ 7$

$4\frac{5}{6}$
$-\ 1\frac{5}{6}$

$1\frac{7}{9}$
$-\ 1\frac{4}{9}$

$6\frac{9}{10}$
$+\ 2\frac{7}{10}$

**5.**
$2\frac{8}{10}$
$+\ 3\frac{5}{10}$

$9\frac{3}{16}$
$-\ 5\frac{1}{16}$

$6\frac{1}{5}$
$+\ 1\frac{2}{5}$

$2\frac{5}{8}$
$+\ 4\frac{3}{8}$

$3\frac{3}{4}$
$-\ 1\frac{1}{4}$

www.summerbridgeactivities.com   **Math Connection—Grade 6—RBP0180**

# Fractions: Renaming and Subtracting Like Denominators

You may need to rename a mixed number before you subtract.

**Example:** $7\frac{1}{9} - 2\frac{4}{9}$

### Step 1

Since $\frac{4}{9} > \frac{1}{9}$, rename $7\frac{1}{9}$

$$7\frac{1}{9} = 6 + \frac{9}{9} + \frac{1}{9} = 6\frac{10}{9}$$
$$-2\frac{4}{9} \qquad\qquad\qquad -2\frac{4}{9}$$

### Step 2

Subtract and write the difference in simplest form.

$$6\frac{10}{9}$$
$$-2\frac{4}{9}$$
$$\overline{4\frac{6}{9} = 4\frac{2}{3}}$$

## Write each difference in simplest form.

**1.**

$7\frac{4}{9}$   $2\frac{5}{8}$   $5\frac{1}{6}$   $7\frac{1}{4}$   $14\frac{3}{5}$

$-2\frac{4}{9}$   $-\frac{7}{8}$   $-2\frac{5}{6}$   $-3\frac{3}{4}$   $-8\frac{4}{5}$

**2.**

$4\frac{3}{7}$   $6\frac{4}{15}$   $8\frac{2}{5}$   $7\frac{3}{8}$   $16\frac{6}{8}$

$-1\frac{5}{7}$   $-4\frac{7}{15}$   $-3\frac{4}{5}$   $-1\frac{5}{8}$   $-9\frac{7}{8}$

**3.**

$9$   $6$   $5$   $4$   $8$

$-3\frac{2}{8}$   $-1\frac{1}{2}$   $-2\frac{3}{4}$   $-1\frac{7}{8}$   $-3\frac{1}{5}$

**4.**

$24$   $20\frac{3}{5}$   $16$   $30\frac{5}{9}$   $18\frac{3}{9}$

$-17\frac{2}{3}$   $-19\frac{4}{5}$   $-13\frac{6}{8}$   $-18\frac{7}{9}$   $-4\frac{7}{9}$

**5.**

$9\frac{4}{15}$   $7\frac{8}{15}$   $8\frac{7}{16}$   $9\frac{7}{12}$   $7\frac{1}{18}$

$-5\frac{10}{15}$   $-3\frac{12}{15}$   $-4\frac{14}{16}$   $-3\frac{11}{12}$   $-1\frac{6}{18}$

# Fractions: Subtracting with Improper Fractions

Another way you can subtract mixed numbers without having to rename them is to change them to improper fractions.

**Example:**

Change to improper fractions → $4\frac{1}{4} = \frac{17}{4}$ ← Subtract the numerators. Simplify.

$-1\frac{3}{4} = -\frac{7}{4}$

$\frac{10}{4} = 2\frac{2}{4} = 2\frac{1}{2}$

## Subtract by changing the mixed numbers to improper fractions.

Simplify your answer. The first problem has been done for you.

**1.**

$8\frac{1}{5} = \frac{41}{5}$
$-3\frac{4}{5} = -\frac{19}{5}$
$\frac{22}{5} = 4\frac{2}{5}$

$6\frac{1}{8} = \frac{\phantom{0}}{8}$
$-1\frac{2}{8} = -\frac{\phantom{0}}{8}$

$9\frac{1}{9} = \frac{\phantom{0}}{9}$
$-3\frac{6}{9} = -\frac{\phantom{0}}{9}$

**2.**

$5\frac{2}{5} =$
$-2\frac{3}{5} =$

$4\frac{2}{8} =$
$-3\frac{6}{8} =$

$7\frac{2}{4} =$
$-4\frac{3}{4} =$

**3.**

$10\frac{3}{8} =$
$-6\frac{5}{8} =$

$6\frac{3}{6} =$
$-2\frac{5}{6} =$

$14\frac{2}{6} =$
$-4\frac{4}{6} =$

**4.**

$14\frac{3}{5} =$
$-8\frac{4}{5} =$

$16\frac{6}{8} =$
$-9\frac{7}{8} =$

$14\frac{2}{5} =$
$-4\frac{4}{5} =$

www.summerbridgeactivities.com Math Connection—Grade 6—RBP0180

## Fractions: Adding and Subtracting Fractions with Unlike Denominators

When you add or subtract fractions with unlike denominators, it helps to think of a model of the fractions.

$$\frac{5}{6} + \frac{3}{4} = \frac{10}{12} + \frac{9}{12}$$

Write equivalent fractions with the lowest common denominator. Then add or subtract the numerator. Simplify your answer.

$$\frac{5}{6} = \frac{10}{12}$$
$$+\frac{3}{4} = +\frac{9}{12}$$
$$\frac{19}{12} = 1\frac{7}{12}$$

It's like adding apples and oranges!

$$\frac{4}{5} = \frac{24}{30}$$
$$+\frac{2}{6} = -\frac{10}{30}$$
$$\frac{14}{30} = \frac{7}{15}$$

## Add or subtract. Write the answer in simplest form.

**1.**   $\frac{2}{3}$   $+\frac{1}{4}$    $\frac{5}{6}$   $-\frac{4}{9}$    $\frac{2}{5}$   $+\frac{7}{10}$    $\frac{3}{5}$   $-\frac{1}{4}$    $\frac{4}{9}$   $+\frac{2}{3}$

**2.**   $\frac{3}{8}$   $+\frac{5}{6}$    $\frac{1}{2}$   $+\frac{7}{8}$    $\frac{2}{3}$   $-\frac{3}{5}$    $\frac{3}{10}$   $+\frac{3}{4}$    $\frac{5}{6}$   $-\frac{1}{7}$

**3.**   $\frac{1}{2}$   $-\frac{3}{10}$    $\frac{1}{2}$   $+\frac{4}{5}$    $\frac{3}{10}$   $-\frac{1}{6}$    $\frac{2}{3}$   $+\frac{5}{9}$    $\frac{1}{8}$   $+\frac{4}{5}$

**4.**   $\frac{1}{6}$   $-\frac{1}{12}$    $\frac{2}{15}$   $+\frac{1}{6}$    $\frac{5}{12}$   $-\frac{1}{4}$    $\frac{4}{7}$   $+\frac{6}{9}$    $\frac{6}{7}$   $-\frac{2}{5}$

**5.**   $\frac{10}{15}$   $-\frac{2}{6}$    $\frac{4}{8}$   $-\frac{7}{16}$    $\frac{8}{10}$   $-\frac{1}{5}$    $\frac{4}{15}$   $+\frac{6}{10}$    $\frac{9}{16}$   $-\frac{16}{32}$

# Fractions: Adding and Subtracting Fractions with Unlike Denominators

| **Step 1** Write equivalent fractions with the lowest common denominator. | **Step 2** Add or subtract the numerators of the fraction part. | **Step 3** Add or subtract the whole numbers. | **Step 4** Simplify. |
|---|---|---|---|
| $4\frac{5}{6} = 4\frac{15}{18}$ <br> $-1\frac{3}{9} = -1\frac{6}{18}$ | $4\frac{15}{18}$ <br> $-1\frac{6}{18}$ <br> $\frac{9}{18}$ | $4\frac{15}{18}$ <br> $-1\frac{6}{18}$ <br> $3\frac{9}{18}$ | $4\frac{15}{18}$ <br> $-1\frac{6}{18}$ <br> $3\frac{9}{18} = 3\frac{1}{2}$ |

## Add or subtract. Write the answer in simplest form.

**1.**  $4\frac{1}{10}$  $+3\frac{1}{2}$   |   $7\frac{5}{4}$  $+5\frac{1}{6}$   |   $6\frac{7}{8}$  $+2\frac{3}{4}$   |   $9\frac{3}{4}$  $+7\frac{2}{5}$   |   $2\frac{3}{4}$  $+1\frac{1}{6}$

**2.**  $12\frac{7}{8}$  $-6\frac{1}{3}$   |   $36\frac{1}{2}$  $-25\frac{3}{10}$   |   $15\frac{5}{9}$  $-9\frac{1}{3}$   |   $6\frac{10}{18}$  $-2\frac{2}{9}$   |   $8\frac{2}{3}$  $-5\frac{1}{4}$

**3.**  $12\frac{7}{8}$  $+6\frac{1}{3}$   |   $9\frac{7}{8}$  $+4\frac{5}{6}$   |   $8\frac{1}{10}$  $+5\frac{1}{4}$   |   $15\frac{3}{4}$  $+12\frac{5}{8}$   |   $13\frac{5}{6}$  $+11\frac{3}{4}$

**4.**  $8\frac{3}{8}$  $-5\frac{1}{6}$   |   $6\frac{3}{5}$  $-2\frac{1}{4}$   |   $4\frac{1}{2}$  $-2\frac{1}{3}$   |   $5\frac{3}{4}$  $-2\frac{2}{5}$   |   $9\frac{7}{8}$  $-4\frac{5}{6}$

**5.**  $11\frac{4}{5}$  $+24\frac{2}{3}$   |   $6\frac{3}{7}$  $+9\frac{2}{4}$   |   $4\frac{4}{9}$  $+10\frac{3}{4}$   |   $8\frac{4}{9}$  $+7\frac{1}{4}$   |   $12\frac{6}{12}$  $+19\frac{1}{3}$

**6.**  $12\frac{2}{7}$  $-7\frac{1}{3}$   |   $9\frac{8}{15}$  $-6\frac{1}{5}$   |   $18\frac{6}{7}$  $-7\frac{10}{14}$   |   $27\frac{5}{12}$  $-14\frac{1}{3}$   |   $7\frac{6}{10}$  $-3\frac{1}{5}$

# Fractions: Adding and Subtracting Fractions with Unlike Denominators

**Step 1**
Determine the lowest common denominator.

$$8\frac{1}{6} = 8\frac{3}{18}$$
$$-3\frac{5}{6} = -3\frac{15}{18}$$

The LCD is **18**.

**Step 2**
Rename $8\frac{3}{18}$

$$8\frac{3}{18} = 7 + \mathbf{1} + \frac{3}{18}$$
$$= 7 + \frac{18}{18} + \frac{3}{18}$$
$$= 7 + \frac{21}{18}$$
$$= 7\frac{21}{18}$$

**Step 3**
Subtract. Simplify if you can.

$$7\frac{21}{18}$$
$$-3\frac{15}{18}$$
$$4\frac{6}{18} = 4\frac{1}{3}$$

## Add or subtract. Write the answer in simplest form.

1.
$6\frac{1}{4}$
$-4\frac{7}{16}$

$7\frac{1}{7}$
$-3\frac{6}{14}$

$8\frac{1}{3}$
$-2\frac{9}{15}$

$8\frac{1}{4}$
$-4\frac{6}{8}$

2.
$9\frac{1}{18}$
$-5\frac{3}{6}$

$3\frac{1}{10}$
$-1\frac{4}{5}$

$5\frac{1}{16}$
$-4\frac{6}{8}$

$9\frac{2}{5}$
$-5\frac{3}{4}$

3.
$17\frac{2}{6}$
$-2\frac{9}{18}$

$14\frac{3}{8}$
$-1\frac{8}{16}$

$18\frac{2}{6}$
$-5\frac{9}{15}$

$12\frac{1}{6}$
$-8\frac{4}{7}$

4.
$23\frac{1}{10}$
$-11\frac{4}{5}$

$19\frac{2}{4}$
$-14\frac{10}{12}$

$32\frac{7}{16}$
$-20\frac{3}{4}$

$9\frac{6}{15}$
$-4\frac{4}{5}$

5.
$26\frac{2}{16}$
$-17\frac{7}{8}$

$28\frac{7}{12}$
$-19\frac{5}{6}$

$13\frac{12}{20}$
$-12\frac{4}{5}$

$12\frac{1}{16}$
$-1\frac{3}{4}$

Math Connection—Grade 6—RBP0180          www.summerbridgeactivities.com          ©RBP Books

# Fractions: Subtraction Skills Practice

What do you get when the post office burns down?

To find out, subtract. Remember to write your answer in simplest form. Match each letter to its answer in the blanks below. Some answers are not used.

**K** $\dfrac{7}{8}$
$-\dfrac{3}{8}$

**D** $\dfrac{10}{16}$
$-\dfrac{8}{16}$

**L** $4\dfrac{5}{6}$
$-2\dfrac{1}{6}$

**O** $14\dfrac{12}{15}$
$-7\dfrac{11}{15}$

**R** $9$
$-\dfrac{4}{7}$

**A** $8$
$-\dfrac{10}{12}$

**F** $6$
$-2\dfrac{6}{8}$

**H** $12$
$-7\dfrac{10}{18}$

**B** $6\dfrac{3}{5}$
$-4\dfrac{4}{5}$

**M** $9\dfrac{2}{6}$
$-5\dfrac{5}{6}$

**C** $10\dfrac{7}{12}$
$-7\dfrac{9}{12}$

**N** $24\dfrac{6}{16}$
$-17\dfrac{10}{16}$

**S** $\dfrac{5}{9}$
$-\dfrac{1}{3}$

**F** $\dfrac{4}{5}$
$-\dfrac{3}{4}$

**G** $\dfrac{10}{15}$
$-\dfrac{3}{5}$

**E** $\dfrac{12}{16}$
$-\dfrac{3}{8}$

**T** $8\dfrac{1}{3}$
$-6\dfrac{6}{9}$

**L** $14\dfrac{2}{5}$
$-9\dfrac{3}{4}$

**I** $6\dfrac{6}{10}$
$-5\dfrac{4}{5}$

**P** $24\dfrac{3}{8}$
$-16\dfrac{14}{16}$

$\dfrac{}{7\frac{1}{6}}$ $\dfrac{}{2\frac{5}{6}}$ $\dfrac{}{7\frac{1}{6}}$ $\dfrac{}{\frac{2}{9}}$ $\dfrac{}{\frac{3}{8}}$ $\dfrac{}{\quad}$ $\dfrac{}{7\frac{1}{15}}$ $\dfrac{}{\frac{1}{20}}$

$\dfrac{}{1\frac{4}{5}}$ $\dfrac{}{2\frac{2}{3}}$ $\dfrac{}{7\frac{1}{6}}$ $\dfrac{}{2\frac{5}{6}}$ $\dfrac{}{\frac{1}{2}}$ $\dfrac{}{3\frac{1}{2}}$ $\dfrac{}{7\frac{1}{6}}$ $\dfrac{}{\frac{4}{5}}$ $\dfrac{}{2\frac{2}{3}}$

www.summerbridgeactivities.com          Math Connection—Grade 6—RBP0180

# Fractions: Addition and Subtraction Practice with Magic Squares

When you add the numbers in each row, column, and diagonal of a magic square, the sums are the same. Find the missing numbers in each magic square below. The magic sums are given.

| | | |
|---|---|---|
| $1\frac{4}{5}$ | | $2\frac{3}{5}$ |
| | $1\frac{1}{2}$ | |
| | $2\frac{9}{10}$ | $1\frac{1}{5}$ |

The magic sum is $4\frac{1}{2}$.

| | | |
|---|---|---|
| $\frac{4}{15}$ | | $\frac{8}{15}$ |
| | $\frac{1}{3}$ | |
| $\frac{2}{15}$ | | $\frac{2}{5}$ |

The magic sum is 1.

| | | |
|---|---|---|
| $1\frac{1}{8}$ | | $1\frac{3}{8}$ |
| | | |
| $1\frac{1}{4}$ | | $1\frac{1}{2}$ |

The magic sum is $3\frac{15}{16}$.

| | | |
|---|---|---|
| $2\frac{1}{3}$ | | $2\frac{4}{9}$ |
| | | |
| $2\frac{1}{9}$ | | $2\frac{2}{9}$ |

The magic sum is $6\frac{5}{6}$.

Math Connection—Grade 6—RBP0180     www.summerbridgeactivities.com     ©RBP Books

# Fractions: Problem Solving Practice

## Use the information in the recipe to solve each problem.

Write answers in simplest form.

> **Trail Mix Recipe**
>
> $1\frac{1}{4}$ cup sunflower seeds
>
> $1\frac{1}{2}$ cup peanuts
>
> $\frac{3}{4}$ cup candy-coated chocolate pieces
>
> $\frac{5}{8}$ cup raisins
>
> Makes 1 batch.

1. Mrs. Johnson plans to make a batch of trail mix using more raisins than the recipe calls for. If she doubles the amount of raisins, how many cups of raisins will she need?

> **Think:**
> This is a multistep problem.

2. After measuring the amount of peanuts needed to make a batch of trail mix, Mrs. Johnson had $2\frac{1}{2}$ cups of peanuts left over. How many cups of peanuts did she begin with?

3. Ellen Johnson increased the amount of candy-coated chocolate pieces in the recipe to $1\frac{1}{8}$ cups. How many more cups of chocolate pieces did she use than the recipe called for?

4. How many cups of trail mix does one batch make after all the ingredients are added together if none of the measurements are altered?

5. The Johnson family made enough trail mix to take on their hike. They hiked $4\frac{3}{8}$ miles to Green River Gulch and then walked another $1\frac{9}{16}$ miles down the river bank. How far did they hike altogether?

6. Sam and Ellen Johnson hiked an extra $\frac{18}{5}$ miles on an advanced trail. Write the extra distance they hiked as a mixed number.

# Fractions: Problem Solving

1. In a baseball game, the starting pitcher pitched 5 innings. The relief pitcher pitched another $1\frac{2}{3}$ innings before the closing pitcher came in to finish the game.

   **a.** How many more innings did the starting pitcher pitch than the relief pitcher?

   **b.** How many innings had the closing pitcher pitched after he finished the ninth inning?

2. In a city baseball league, the Tigers are $1\frac{1}{2}$ games behind the Pirates, and the Pirates are 4 games ahead of the Cubs. How many games separate the Tigers and the Cubs?

   **Clue:**
   Draw a diagram.

3. Softball bats are $2\frac{1}{2}$ inches in diameter. If a softball is $3\frac{1}{8}$ inches in diameter, how much wider is the softball than the bat?

4. Suppose $\frac{5}{8}$ of major league baseball fans watch the games on television, and $\frac{1}{3}$ of the fans listen to them on the radio. How many more baseball fans watch television than listen to the radio?

5. Bob spent $\frac{3}{8}$ of his birthday money at a baseball game and $\frac{5}{12}$ on a new bat and glove. What fraction of his birthday money did Bob spend?

6. If a baseball game lasted $3\frac{1}{4}$ hours and ended at 10 P.M., at what time did it start?

   **Clue:**
   Work backwards.

www.summerbridgeactivities.com

# Post-Test: Adding and Subtracting Fractions

## Write an improper fraction for each mixed number.

1. $1\frac{2}{5}$ $\qquad$ $5\frac{3}{4}$ $\qquad$ $3\frac{5}{6}$ $\qquad$ $12\frac{7}{8}$

## Write a mixed number or whole number for each fraction.

2. $\frac{28}{5}$ $\qquad$ $\frac{38}{6}$ $\qquad$ $\frac{27}{9}$ $\qquad$ $\frac{48}{10}$

## Add or subtract. Write all answers in simplest form.

3. 
$$\frac{3}{7} + \frac{2}{7}$$
$$\frac{5}{6} + \frac{3}{6}$$
$$\frac{3}{4} + \frac{2}{5}$$
$$\frac{21}{25} + \frac{2}{10}$$

4. 
$$\frac{6}{7} - \frac{3}{7}$$
$$\frac{3}{4} - \frac{1}{3}$$
$$\frac{9}{12} - \frac{3}{5}$$
$$\frac{3}{5} - \frac{2}{9}$$

5. 
$$6\frac{1}{4} + 2\frac{3}{4}$$
$$3\frac{3}{5} + 4\frac{7}{10}$$
$$8\frac{7}{8} + 9\frac{1}{2}$$
$$12\frac{1}{8} + 7\frac{8}{12}$$

6. 
$$7\frac{3}{5} - 2\frac{1}{5}$$
$$8\frac{13}{14} - 5\frac{4}{7}$$
$$6\frac{1}{9} - 1\frac{5}{8}$$
$$18\frac{4}{9} - 9\frac{6}{9}$$

## Solve each problem. Write all answers in simplest form.

7. Rita's video collection consists of $\frac{1}{3}$ comedy videos and $\frac{1}{5}$ adventure videos. What part of Rita's video collection is neither comedy nor adventure videos?

8. A total of 4 inches of rain were predicted for the month of June, but only $2\frac{3}{8}$ inches actually fell. What is the difference between the predicted rainfall and the actual rainfall?

www.summerbridgeactivities.com

# Number Patterns

A **number pattern** is a list of numbers that occur in some predictable way. Many patterns use addition and subtraction. To find the pattern, write the number that you need to add or subtract to find the next number in the pattern.

---

**Example:**

Find the next three numbers in this pattern: **1**, **7**, **2**, **8**, **3**, **9**, **4**, …

**Step 1**
Determine the pattern by writing the number you must add or subtract to get the next number.

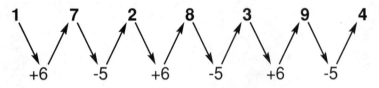

The pattern is **add 6**, **subtract 5**.

**Step 2**
Use the pattern to calculate the next three numbers.

$4 + 6 = 10$   $10 - 5 = 5$

$5 + 6 = 11$

The next three numbers in the pattern are **10**, **5**, and **11**.

---

## Find the next three numbers in each number pattern.

1.   5, 8, 11, 14, 17, ____, ____, ____          7, 15, 23, 31, 39, ____, ____, ____

2.   91, 86, 81, 76, 71, ____, ____, ____          100, 92, 84, 76, 68, ____, ____, ____

3.   10, 20, 25, 35, 40, ____, ____, ____          99, 86, 73, 60, 47, ____, ____, ____

4.   317, 402, 487, 572, ____, ____, ____          5, 11, 23, 47, 95, ____, ____, ____

5.   244, 226, 208, 190, ____, ____, ____          1, 4, 9, 16, 25, ____, ____, ____

6.   1, 2, 4, 8, 16, ____, ____, ____          53, 54, 56, 59, 63, ____, ____, ____

7.   30, 34, 40, 48, 58, ____, ____, ____          99, 88, 77, 66, ____, ____, ____

8.   11, 16, 14, 19, 17, ____, ____, ____          19, 34, 49, 64, 79, ____, ____, ____

# Pre-Test: Multiplying Fractions

## Multiply. Write each fraction or mixed number in simplest form.

1.  $\dfrac{1}{4} \times \dfrac{1}{4} =$       $\dfrac{3}{10} \times \dfrac{1}{12} =$       $\dfrac{4}{7} \times \dfrac{2}{3} =$       $\dfrac{3}{4} \times \dfrac{6}{8} =$

2.  $\dfrac{3}{4} \times \dfrac{6}{5} =$       $\dfrac{3}{7} \times \dfrac{4}{5} =$       $\dfrac{2}{3} \times 9 =$       $\dfrac{4}{6} \times 7 =$

3.  $4 \times \dfrac{10}{16} =$       $\dfrac{10}{15} \times 3 =$       $\dfrac{3}{4} \times 2\dfrac{3}{5} =$       $\dfrac{2}{3} \times 3\dfrac{2}{6} =$

4.  $1\dfrac{3}{9} \times \dfrac{2}{3} =$       $1\dfrac{2}{8} \times \dfrac{2}{4} =$       $2\dfrac{1}{4} \times 3\dfrac{1}{5} =$       $1\dfrac{1}{3} \times 1\dfrac{1}{6} =$

5.  $2\dfrac{3}{5} \times 1\dfrac{2}{3} =$       $3\dfrac{3}{4} \times 2\dfrac{3}{5} =$       $2\dfrac{1}{3} \times 6 =$       $1\dfrac{4}{16} \times 4 =$

## Solve each problem.

6. Sterling travels $2\dfrac{1}{8}$ miles each day on his paper route. How many miles does he travel in 5 days?

7. Sterling delivers 35 newspapers, of which $\dfrac{2}{5}$ are delivered on his street. How many newspapers does he deliver on his street?

www.summerbridgeactivities.com   Math Connection—Grade 6—RBP0180

# Fractions: Multiplication

To multiply fractions:

Multiply $\frac{3}{4} \times \frac{2}{8}$

**Step 1**
Multiply the numerators.
Multiply the denominators.

$$\frac{3}{4} \times \frac{2}{8} = \frac{3 \times 2}{4 \times 8}$$
$$= \frac{6}{32}$$

**Step 2**
Write the fraction in simplest form.

$$\frac{6 \div 2}{32 \div 2} = \frac{3}{16}$$

## Multiply. Write each fraction in simplest form.

1. $\frac{1}{8} \times \frac{1}{5} =$ 　　 $\frac{1}{4} \times \frac{1}{7} =$ 　　 $\frac{1}{12} \times \frac{1}{8} =$ 　　 $\frac{1}{15} \times \frac{1}{10} =$

2. $\frac{3}{7} \times \frac{4}{5} =$ 　　 $\frac{4}{5} \times \frac{6}{8} =$ 　　 $\frac{2}{3} \times \frac{4}{7} =$ 　　 $\frac{6}{8} \times \frac{3}{4} =$

3. $\frac{5}{6} \times \frac{4}{5} =$ 　　 $\frac{2}{3} \times \frac{7}{8} =$ 　　 $\frac{7}{9} \times \frac{8}{9} =$ 　　 $\frac{9}{10} \times \frac{2}{3} =$

4. $\frac{1}{2} \times \frac{2}{12} =$ 　　 $\frac{2}{3} \times \frac{4}{12} =$ 　　 $\frac{6}{8} \times \frac{4}{16} =$ 　　 $\frac{9}{15} \times \frac{5}{6} =$

5. $\frac{7}{10} \times \frac{3}{5} =$ 　　 $\frac{2}{7} \times \frac{10}{14} =$ 　　 $\frac{4}{6} \times \frac{12}{18} =$ 　　 $\frac{4}{5} \times \frac{10}{12} =$

6. $\frac{12}{16} \times \frac{3}{7} =$ 　　 $\frac{6}{12} \times \frac{5}{6} =$ 　　 $\frac{2}{4} \times \frac{10}{12} =$ 　　 $\frac{2}{3} \times \frac{3}{7} =$

# Fractions: Multiplication

To multiply a fraction by a whole number:

Multiply $\frac{2}{3} \times 4$

| **Step 1** | **Step 2** | **Step 3** |
|---|---|---|
| Write the whole number as a fraction. | Multiply the numerators. Multiply the denominators. | Change the fraction to a mixed number whose fraction is in simplest form. |
| $\frac{2}{3} \times 4 = \frac{2}{3} \times \frac{4}{1}$ | $\frac{2}{3} \times \frac{4}{1} = \frac{2 \times 4}{3 \times 1}$ <br> $= \frac{8}{3}$ | $\frac{8}{3} = 2\frac{2}{3}$ |

 Any whole number can be turned into a fraction by writing a 1 as the denominator.

## Multiply. Write each fraction in simplest form.

1.    $\frac{1}{15} \times 5 =$      $\frac{5}{14} \times 7 =$      $\frac{1}{16} \times 8 =$      $\frac{7}{12} \times 3 =$

2.    $\frac{6}{15} \times 4 =$      $\frac{5}{12} \times 6 =$      $\frac{3}{16} \times 8 =$      $\frac{6}{10} \times 5 =$

3.    $\frac{9}{12} \times 3 =$      $\frac{4}{18} \times 6 =$      $\frac{5}{15} \times 10 =$      $\frac{4}{12} \times 12 =$

4.    $2 \times \frac{9}{10} =$      $6 \times \frac{3}{18} =$      $4 \times \frac{6}{16} =$      $6 \times \frac{3}{17} =$

5.    $3 \times \frac{4}{15} =$      $5 \times \frac{10}{12} =$      $5 \times \frac{3}{6} =$      $4 \times \frac{5}{16} =$

6.    $3 \times \frac{5}{11} =$      $2 \times \frac{7}{12} =$      $2 \times \frac{12}{13} =$      $4 \times \frac{11}{16} =$

# Fractions: Multiplication

To multiply a fraction by a mixed number:

Multiply $\frac{3}{4} \times 1\frac{4}{5}$

---

**Step 1**
Write the mixed number as an improper fraction.

$$\frac{3}{4} \times 1\frac{4}{5} = \frac{3}{4} \times \frac{9}{5}$$

**Step 2**
Multiply the numerators.
Multiply the denominators.

$$\frac{3}{4} \times \frac{9}{5} = \frac{3 \times 9}{4 \times 5}$$
$$= \frac{27}{20}$$

**Step 3**
Change the fraction answer to a mixed number whose fraction is in simplest form.

$$\frac{27}{20} = 1\frac{7}{20}$$

**Think:** Is this fraction in simplest form?

---

## Multiply. Write each fraction in simplest form.

1.    $\frac{1}{3} \times 3\frac{1}{4} =$      $\frac{1}{2} \times 2\frac{1}{5} =$      $\frac{2}{4} \times 2\frac{1}{6} =$      $\frac{2}{5} \times 3\frac{1}{2} =$

2.    $\frac{3}{6} \times 4\frac{3}{4} =$      $\frac{4}{8} \times 5\frac{2}{3} =$      $6\frac{1}{3} \times \frac{1}{8} =$      $7\frac{1}{4} \times \frac{1}{9} =$

3.    $2\frac{3}{4} \times \frac{3}{5} =$      $4\frac{2}{5} \times \frac{3}{4} =$      $1\frac{2}{7} \times \frac{2}{4} =$      $3\frac{2}{8} \times \frac{2}{3} =$

4.    $\frac{1}{10} \times 5\frac{1}{4} =$      $\frac{1}{5} \times 4\frac{1}{2} =$      $\frac{2}{15} \times 10\frac{2}{4} =$      $\frac{4}{9} \times 3\frac{2}{3} =$

5.    $7\frac{1}{2} \times \frac{1}{12} =$      $3\frac{1}{4} \times \frac{1}{13} =$      $2\frac{3}{4} \times \frac{2}{11} =$      $3\frac{2}{5} \times \frac{3}{10} =$

6.    $\frac{3}{11} \times 2\frac{2}{8} =$      $\frac{4}{10} \times 3\frac{2}{6} =$      $\frac{4}{15} \times 1\frac{5}{8} =$      $\frac{1}{15} \times 1\frac{8}{10} =$

---

# Fractions: Multiplication

To multiply two mixed numbers:

Multiply $1\frac{2}{3} \times 4\frac{2}{5}$

| **Step 1** Write each mixed number as an improper fraction. | **Step 2** Multiply the numerators. Multiply the denominators. | **Step 3** Change the fraction answer to a mixed number whose fraction is in simplest form. |
|---|---|---|
| $1\frac{2}{3} = \frac{5}{3}$ $4\frac{2}{5} = \frac{22}{5}$ | $\frac{5}{3} \times \frac{22}{5} = \frac{5 \times 22}{3 \times 5}$ $= \frac{110}{15}$ | $\frac{110}{15} = 7\frac{5}{15} = 7\frac{1}{3}$ |

## Multiply. Write each answer as a fraction or a mixed number in simplest form.

1.  $3\frac{1}{3} \times 4\frac{1}{40} =$    $2\frac{1}{5} \times 1\frac{1}{6} =$    $2\frac{1}{4} \times 2\frac{1}{2} =$    $1\frac{2}{3} \times 2\frac{4}{5} =$

2.  $1\frac{1}{6} \times 2\frac{1}{7} =$    $4\frac{1}{8} \times 1\frac{1}{8} =$    $3\frac{1}{2} \times 3\frac{3}{4} =$    $1\frac{1}{6} \times 2\frac{2}{3} =$

3.  $1\frac{1}{4} \times 3\frac{2}{5} =$    $2\frac{1}{3} \times 1\frac{6}{8} =$    $2\frac{4}{5} \times 3\frac{1}{6} =$    $1\frac{3}{9} \times 1\frac{1}{4} =$

4.  $3\frac{2}{8} \times 1\frac{1}{2} =$    $2\frac{3}{7} \times 2\frac{1}{4} =$    $1\frac{2}{7} \times 2\frac{2}{5} =$    $2\frac{3}{8} \times 1\frac{2}{3} =$

5.  $2\frac{3}{5} \times 3\frac{2}{4} =$    $1\frac{2}{9} \times 1\frac{3}{5} =$    $1\frac{1}{16} \times 2\frac{1}{4} =$    $2\frac{2}{10} \times 1\frac{1}{2} =$

6.  $1\frac{3}{7} \times 2\frac{2}{5} =$    $1\frac{6}{8} \times 2\frac{2}{5} =$    $1\frac{1}{12} \times 1\frac{1}{3} =$    $1\frac{3}{15} \times 1\frac{1}{2} =$

# Fractions: Multiplication

To multiply a whole number by a mixed number:

Multiply $5 \times 6\frac{4}{7}$

| **Step 1** | **Step 2** | **Step 3** |
|---|---|---|
| Write both numbers as fractions. | Multiply the numerators. Multiply the denominators. | Change the fraction answer to a mixed number. Simplify. |

**Step 1**

$5 = \dfrac{5}{1}$ $\qquad 6\frac{4}{7} = \dfrac{46}{7}$

↑

Remember to write the denominator as 1.

**Step 2**

$\dfrac{5}{1} \times \dfrac{46}{7} = \dfrac{5 \times 46}{1 \times 7}$

$\qquad\qquad = \dfrac{230}{7}$

**Step 3**

$\dfrac{230}{7} = 32\frac{6}{7}$

$$
\begin{array}{r}
32\frac{6}{7} \\
7\overline{)230} \\
-21\phantom{0} \\
\hline
20 \\
-14 \\
\hline
6
\end{array}
$$

## Multiply. Write each answer as a fraction or a mixed number in simplest form.

1. $6 \times 2\frac{1}{3} =$ $\qquad$ $7 \times 2\frac{1}{5} =$ $\qquad$ $3 \times 2\frac{3}{5} =$ $\qquad$ $8 \times 1\frac{4}{9} =$

2. $2 \times 1\frac{3}{8} =$ $\qquad$ $5 \times 4\frac{2}{4} =$ $\qquad$ $6 \times 2\frac{4}{5} =$ $\qquad$ $4 \times 1\frac{2}{7} =$

3. $2\frac{1}{3} \times 3 =$ $\qquad$ $1\frac{1}{8} \times 5 =$ $\qquad$ $1\frac{1}{4} \times 6 =$ $\qquad$ $2\frac{1}{5} \times 4 =$

4. $3\frac{3}{7} \times 2 =$ $\qquad$ $2\frac{4}{5} \times 3 =$ $\qquad$ $2\frac{3}{4} \times 4 =$ $\qquad$ $1\frac{2}{8} \times 5 =$

5. $1\frac{3}{9} \times 5 =$ $\qquad$ $1\frac{5}{8} \times 2 =$ $\qquad$ $6 \times 2\frac{2}{5} =$ $\qquad$ $7 \times 3\frac{3}{4} =$

6. $8 \times 3\frac{1}{5} =$ $\qquad$ $1\frac{2}{7} \times 3 =$ $\qquad$ $2\frac{2}{3} \times 6 =$ $\qquad$ $1\frac{4}{16} \times 6 =$

# Fractions: Taking a Fraction of a Number

In mathematics the word **of** is the same as **times**.

**Example:**

What is $\frac{2}{3}$ of **51**?

This is the same as asking

what is $\frac{2}{3} \times 51$?

Remember **of** means **x**.

$\frac{2}{3} \times 51 = \frac{2}{3} \times \frac{51}{1}$    Turn the whole number into a fraction by writing a 1 as the denominator.

$= \frac{2 \times 51}{3 \times 1}$    Multiply the numerators. Multiply the denominators.

$= \frac{102}{3}$

$= 3\overline{)102}$    Remember that the fraction bar is also a division bar.

$= 34$    So, $\frac{2}{3}$ of 51 is 34.

## Multiply. Write each answer as a fraction or a mixed number in simplest form.

1.  $\frac{2}{5}$ of 10        $\frac{5}{6}$ of 24        $\frac{4}{5}$ of 60        $\frac{3}{4}$ of 44

2.  $\frac{7}{10}$ of 80        $\frac{6}{25}$ of 125        $\frac{5}{8}$ of 96        $\frac{7}{12}$ of 144

3.  $\frac{1}{2}$ of 15        $\frac{2}{3}$ of 32        $\frac{3}{4}$ of 78        $\frac{1}{8}$ of 74

4.  $\frac{5}{8}$ of 20        $\frac{1}{3}$ of 22        $\frac{1}{6}$ of 50        $\frac{9}{10}$ of 35

5.  Four-sevenths of the students in Mrs. Mason's 6th grade class are girls. If there are 28 students in Mrs. Mason's class, how many of these are girls? **Think:** What is $\frac{4}{7}$ of 28?

6.  Three-fifths of the cookies on the tray are chocolate chip. If there are 120 cookies on the tray, how many cookies are chocolate chip?

7.  Two-sevenths of the students at Kingston Elementary school are 6th graders. If there are 665 students at Kingston Elementary, how many of these are 6th graders?

## Fractions: Multiplication Practice

**Multiply. Connect the answers from START to FINISH. Circle the correct FINISH.**

1. $\frac{4}{9} \times \frac{3}{8}$

2. $7 \times \frac{5}{7}$

3. $\frac{3}{12} \times \frac{3}{5}$

4. $2\frac{1}{2} \times \frac{1}{5}$

5. $\frac{2}{3} \times \frac{5}{10}$

6. $\frac{5}{6} \times 8\frac{1}{5}$

7. $\frac{1}{3} \times 8$

8. $\frac{2}{3} \times 6$

9. $3\frac{2}{4} \times 1\frac{2}{7}$

10. $4\frac{1}{8} \times 2\frac{4}{5}$

11. $2\frac{2}{7} \times 3$

12. $4 \times 2\frac{4}{5}$

13. $\frac{2}{9} \times 1\frac{3}{4}$

14. $\frac{2}{12} \times \frac{1}{10}$

15. $2\frac{1}{3} \times 3\frac{5}{6}$

16. $\frac{2}{7} \times \frac{4}{3}$

17. $\frac{1}{4} \times \frac{1}{5}$

18. $2\frac{4}{5} \times \frac{3}{7}$

19. $\frac{5}{8} \times \frac{3}{4}$

20. $2\frac{2}{3} \times 1\frac{3}{5}$

| | | | | | | | |
|---|---|---|---|---|---|---|---|
| $8\frac{11}{18}$ | $\frac{4}{11}$ | $2\frac{2}{3}$ | $4$ | $4\frac{1}{2}$ | $5\frac{9}{10}$ | $\frac{7}{24}$ | FINISH |
| $2\frac{14}{15}$ | $\frac{1}{3}$ | $6\frac{5}{6}$ | $\frac{2}{9}$ | $11\frac{11}{20}$ | $\frac{15}{32}$ | $4\frac{4}{15}$ | FINISH |
| $\frac{7}{15}$ | $\frac{1}{2}$ | $\frac{6}{21}$ | $11\frac{1}{5}$ | $6\frac{6}{7}$ | $1\frac{1}{5}$ | $9\frac{1}{2}$ | FINISH |
| $5$ | $\frac{3}{20}$ | $8\frac{1}{3}$ | $\frac{7}{18}$ | $7$ | $\frac{1}{20}$ | $\frac{2}{3}$ | FINISH |
| START $\frac{1}{6}$ | $\frac{19}{20}$ | $4\frac{1}{4}$ | $\frac{1}{60}$ | $8\frac{17}{18}$ | $\frac{8}{21}$ | $12\frac{5}{8}$ | FINISH |

# Fractions: Multiplication Practice

## BOOKS NEVER WRITTEN

_We've Got to Stop Meeting Like This_     by  _____

$\frac{10}{21}$     $\frac{3}{4}$     $\frac{1}{2}$     $\frac{16}{91}$     $\frac{1}{18}$     $\frac{25}{26}$     $\frac{3}{4}$     $\frac{3}{4}$

_Scuba Diving Safety_     by  _____

$4\frac{5}{16}$     $\frac{1}{3}$     $\frac{2}{9}$     $1\frac{5}{9}$     $\frac{7}{9}$     $\frac{2}{9}$     $\frac{10}{21}$     $2\frac{5}{8}$

_Honesty Is the Best Policy_     by  _____

$10\frac{5}{16}$     $\frac{13}{18}$     $10\frac{5}{16}$     $\frac{1}{18}$     $\frac{3}{4}$     $\frac{9}{14}$     $\frac{9}{14}$

_Friendly Insects_     by  _____

$\frac{2}{9}$     $\frac{1}{3}$     $\frac{3}{4}$     $1\frac{5}{9}$     $2\frac{5}{8}$     $\frac{1}{18}$     $\frac{1}{18}$     $\frac{9}{14}$     $\frac{2}{9}$     $\frac{7}{9}$

Above are the titles of four "BOOKS NEVER WRITTEN." To decode the names of their authors, do the exercises below and find your answer in the code above. Each time the answer appears in the code, write the letter of that exercise above it. Keep working, and you will decode the names of all four authors. Write on!

A $\frac{1}{4} \times \frac{8}{9}$     J $2\frac{1}{6} \times \frac{8}{9}$     S $\frac{2}{3} \times 2\frac{3}{9}$

B $\frac{7}{8} \times \frac{6}{13}$     K $3\frac{3}{8} \times \frac{7}{9}$     T $1\frac{1}{8} \times \frac{4}{7}$

C $\frac{1}{3} \times \frac{9}{11}$     L $7\frac{1}{2} \times 1\frac{3}{8}$     U $4 \times 6\frac{1}{9}$

D $\frac{8}{13} \times \frac{2}{7}$     M $\frac{5}{9} \times \frac{3}{5}$     V $1\frac{12}{13} \times \frac{1}{2}$

E $\frac{2}{3} \times \frac{1}{12}$     N $\frac{5}{6} \times \frac{3}{5}$     W $\frac{3}{4} \times 4\frac{3}{5}$

F $\frac{10}{13} \times \frac{1}{10}$     O $\frac{5}{6} \times \frac{9}{10}$     X $1\frac{3}{5} \times 2$

G $1\frac{4}{5} \times \frac{5}{6}$     P $\frac{4}{5} \times \frac{5}{11}$     Y $3\frac{1}{4} \times \frac{2}{9}$

H $\frac{4}{9} \times 1\frac{3}{4}$     Q $\frac{1}{5} \times \frac{10}{11}$     Z $\frac{5}{7} \times 3\frac{2}{5}$

I $2\frac{7}{8} \times 1\frac{1}{2}$     R $\frac{2}{3} \times \frac{5}{7}$

Wait 'til the critics see these!

## Multiplying Fractions: Problem Solving

### Solve each problem.

1. Carl is making dinner for a group of his friends. He is making a recipe for stuffed chilies that uses $1\frac{3}{4}$ cups of cream cheese. Carl will only need to make $\frac{2}{3}$ of the recipe. How much cream cheese should he use?

2. A 2-serving recipe for chicken mole calls for $3\frac{1}{2}$ teaspoons of chili powder and $1\frac{1}{2}$ tablespoons of olive oil. How much of each ingredient is needed to make 3 servings?

   **Think:** How much of each ingredient is needed for 1 serving?

3. Carl has $\frac{7}{8}$ pounds of cheese. He uses $\frac{1}{7}$ of this in his quesadillas. Since there are 16 ounces in 1 pound, how many ounces of cheese does Carl use in his quesadillas?

   **Think:** What is $\frac{7}{8}$ of 16 ounces? _____   What is $\frac{1}{7}$ of that? _____

## In problems 4–6, solve using this recipe.

| Chillaquillas (Serves 6) | |
| --- | --- |
| 1 dozen tortillas | $\frac{2}{3}$ cup chopped green onions |
| $2\frac{1}{2}$ cups grated jack cheese | $2\frac{1}{4}$ teaspoons chili powder |
| $1\frac{1}{3}$ cups tomato sauce | $\frac{1}{2}$ teaspoon crushed oregano |
| $1\frac{1}{4}$ cups low-fat cottage cheese | $\frac{1}{4}$ cup oil |

**Clue:**
Use logical reasoning.

4. Carl will need enough chillaquillas to serve 8 people. What number should the recipe be multiplied by to make enough for all 8 people?

5. How much tomato sauce is required if the recipe is multiplied by $1\frac{1}{3}$ ?

6. How many cups of chopped green onions will be needed if the recipe is tripled?

7. Challenge: Carl's recipe instructs him to bake at 205°C (degrees Celsius). He can convert this temperature to degrees Fahrenheit (°F) using this formula:

   $$°F = \frac{9}{5} \times °C + 32$$

   What cooking temperature should he use in degrees Fahrenheit?

# Multiplying Fractions: Problem Solving

During Year 2, the water in a pond dries up, and the size of the pond decreases to $\frac{1}{3}$ of what it was in Year 1. Assume that the same decrease occurs during Year 3. What fraction of the pond will remain after Year 3?

**Picture It**  Here is a model of the information.

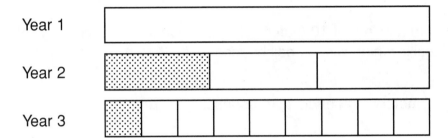

**Solve It**  Use the model to help you solve the problem.

Let 1 represent the whole pond in Year 1.

The size of the pond after Year 2 is $\frac{1}{3}$ the size of the pond in Year 1.
Find the fraction of the pond remaining after Year 2.

$$\frac{1}{3} \times 1 = \frac{1}{3}$$

The size of the pond after Year 3 is $\frac{1}{3}$ the size of the pond after Year 2. Find the fraction of the pond remaining after Year 3.

$$\frac{1}{3} \times \frac{1}{3} = \frac{1}{9}$$

After Year 3, the pond will be $\frac{1}{9}$ the size it had been in Year 1.

## Solve each problem. Draw a model to help you.

1. Suppose every bounce of a ball is 2/3 the height of its previous bounce. What fraction of the original height will the height of Bounce 3 be?

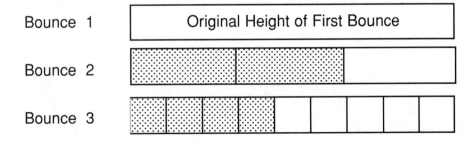

On Bounce 3, the ball will bounce to _____ of its original height.

www.summerbridgeactivities.com                    Math Connection—Grade 6—RBP0180

# Multiplying Fractions: Problem Solving (Continued)

2. Suppose a ball is dropped from its original height of 2 meters. Every bounce of the ball is $\frac{1}{2}$ the height of its previous bounce. How high will the ball bounce on Bounce 3?

   On Bounce 3, the ball will bounce _____ meter high.

3. A different ball is dropped from a height of 10 meters. On each bounce, it reaches $\frac{4}{5}$ of the height of its previous bounce. How high will the ball bounce on its third bounce?

   The ball will bounce _____ meters high on its third bounce.

4. Each month for 8 months, Cameron pays back $\frac{1}{2}$ the remaining money he owes his grandmother. Cameron owes $400. Continue the model to find the first month in which Cameron will pay his grandmother less than $20.

| | | |
|---|---|---|
| Cameron Owes | | $400 |
| Month 1 | | $\frac{1}{2}$ of $400 |

   The first month Cameron will pay his Grandmother less than $20 is month _____.

5. Each day, Tina studies for $\frac{1}{2}$ the number of minutes she did the previous day. If she studied for 32 minutes on Day 1, how many minutes will she study on Day 3?

   Tina will study for _____ minutes on Day 3.

6. An endangered bird species decreases in population size each year. Every year the number of birds is $\frac{2}{3}$ of what it was the previous year. If there were 900 birds in the year 2001, how many birds should there be after the year 2003?

   There should be about _____ birds after the year 2003.

Math Connection—Grade 6—RBP0180          www.summerbridgeactivities.com          ©RBP Books

# Post-Test: Multiplying Fractions

## Multiply. Write each fraction or mixed number in simplest form.

**1.** $\frac{1}{6} \times \frac{4}{5} =$          $\frac{4}{7} \times \frac{1}{3} =$          $\frac{1}{3} \times \frac{5}{7} =$          $\frac{5}{6} \times \frac{3}{7} =$

**2.** $\frac{3}{4} \times \frac{8}{9} =$          $\frac{5}{6} \times \frac{3}{5} =$          $\frac{12}{13} \times \frac{2}{3} =$          $\frac{4}{5} \times \frac{10}{11} =$

**3.** $3 \times \frac{3}{16} =$          $\frac{10}{12} \times 4 =$          $\frac{1}{6} \times 8\frac{3}{4} =$          $\frac{5}{8} \times 5\frac{7}{8} =$

**4.** $1\frac{1}{3} \times \frac{5}{6} =$          $1\frac{1}{5} \times \frac{1}{4} =$          $\frac{2}{5} \times 3\frac{1}{3} =$          $2\frac{2}{9} \times 1\frac{3}{5} =$

**5.** $2\frac{5}{8} \times 5 =$          $4 \times 2\frac{2}{11} =$          $2\frac{1}{4} \times 5\frac{1}{2} =$          $1\frac{3}{11} \times 2\frac{3}{4} =$

## Solve each problem.

**6.** Madeline needs $2\frac{1}{8}$ yards of fabric to make a duffel bag. How much fabric does she need to make 3 duffel bags?

**7.** Tanner can make a small gym bag from $1\frac{1}{8}$ yards of fabric. He needs $1\frac{1}{2}$ times as much fabric to make a large gym bag. How much fabric does Tanner need to make a large gym bag?

# Pre-Test: Dividing Fractions

## Write the reciprocal of the number.

1.  $\frac{2}{3}$          $\frac{7}{4}$          $4\frac{1}{2}$          $5$          $11\frac{1}{3}$

## Divide. Write each fraction or mixed number in simplest form.

2.  $4 \div \frac{1}{6} =$     $3 \div \frac{1}{8} =$     $6 \div \frac{1}{5} =$     $2 \div \frac{3}{8} =$

3.  $5 \div \frac{5}{7} =$     $4 \div \frac{3}{5} =$     $\frac{3}{4} \div \frac{4}{5} =$     $\frac{2}{3} \div \frac{4}{6} =$

4.  $\frac{2}{7} \div \frac{3}{5} =$     $2\frac{2}{3} \div \frac{3}{6} =$     $1\frac{3}{8} \div \frac{2}{4} =$     $2\frac{4}{5} \div \frac{3}{5} =$

5.  $\frac{3}{8} \div 3 =$     $\frac{3}{8} \div 2 =$     $3\frac{3}{5} \div 8 =$     $2\frac{3}{5} \div 4\frac{3}{6} =$

6.  $4\frac{3}{9} \div 2\frac{2}{3} =$     $3\frac{6}{8} \div 2\frac{2}{8} =$     $\frac{4}{5} \div \frac{1}{6} =$     $3\frac{2}{3} \div 2\frac{8}{9} =$

## Solve the equations for _n_.

7.  $n \times \frac{2}{3} = \frac{5}{9}$          $n \div \frac{1}{8} = \frac{1}{6}$

8.  $n \times 2\frac{1}{3} = 10\frac{4}{15}$          $n \div 2\frac{3}{8} = 1\frac{1}{3}$

## Solve the problem.

9. Each bead on Josie's necklace is $\frac{3}{8}$ inch long. All the beads together measure $3\frac{3}{4}$ inches. How many beads are part of her necklace?

# Reciprocals

The number 0 has no reciprocal.

Two numbers are **reciprocals** of each other when their product is **1**.

$\frac{2}{3}$ and $1\frac{1}{2}$ are reciprocals, because $1\frac{1}{2} = \frac{3}{2}$ and $\frac{2}{3} \times \frac{3}{2} = \frac{6}{6}$ or **1**.

$1\frac{3}{4}$ and $\frac{4}{7}$ are reciprocals, because $1\frac{3}{4} = \frac{7}{4}$ and $\frac{7}{4} \times \frac{4}{7} = \frac{28}{28}$ or **1**.

To find the reciprocal of a fraction, reverse the numerator and the denominator.

**Example:** Find the reciprocal of 1/8.

The reciprocal of 1/8 is 8/1, or 8.

Find the reciprocal of 15.

- First write 15 as a fraction. **$15 = \frac{15}{1}$**

- Then reverse the numerator and denominator to find the reciprocal. $\frac{1}{15}$

- Check: $\frac{15}{1} \times \frac{1}{15} = 1$

Find the reciprocal of $4\frac{1}{3}$.

- First write $4\frac{1}{3}$ as an improper fraction.  $4\frac{1}{3} = \frac{13}{3}$

- Then reverse the numerator and denominator. $\frac{3}{13}$

- Check: $\frac{13}{3} \times \frac{3}{13} = 1$

## Find the reciprocal of each number.

| | | | | |
|---|---|---|---|---|
| **1.** $\frac{11}{5}$ | $2\frac{1}{4}$ | 9 | $\frac{3}{10}$ | $8\frac{2}{3}$ |
| **2.** $\frac{1}{7}$ | $4\frac{5}{8}$ | $\frac{15}{11}$ | $\frac{1}{6}$ | $4\frac{1}{2}$ |
| **3.** $\frac{3}{4}$ | 3 | $\frac{9}{4}$ | $7\frac{5}{8}$ | 1 |
| **4.** $5\frac{2}{3}$ | $\frac{7}{9}$ | 27 | $2\frac{1}{5}$ | $3\frac{2}{5}$ |
| **5.** $\frac{1}{3}$ | 22 | $\frac{10}{7}$ | $2\frac{1}{8}$ | $9\frac{7}{8}$ |

## Divide by a Fraction

To find $\frac{4}{5} \div \frac{3}{4}$, multiply $\frac{4}{5}$ by the reciprocal of $\frac{3}{4}$.

Reciprocals

Rewrite $\frac{4}{5} \div \frac{3}{4}$ as $\frac{4}{5} \times \frac{4}{3}$.

Then multiply and simplify: $\frac{4 \times 4}{5 \times 3} = \frac{16}{15} = 1\frac{1}{15}$

So $\frac{4}{5} \div \frac{3}{4} = 1\frac{1}{15}$

## Complete.

1.    $\frac{7}{2} \div \frac{1}{2} = \frac{7}{2} \times \frac{2}{1}$        $\frac{4}{3} \div \frac{2}{3} =$        $\frac{6}{4} \div \frac{3}{4} =$

        $\frac{7}{2} \times \frac{2}{1} = \frac{14}{2} = \frac{7}{1}$       $\frac{4}{3} \times \frac{3}{2} =$        $\frac{6}{4} \times \frac{4}{3} =$

2.    $\frac{9}{2} \div \frac{1}{3} =$            $\frac{8}{3} \div \frac{2}{5} =$        $\frac{15}{4} \div \frac{3}{7} =$

        $\frac{9}{2} \times \frac{3}{1} =$            $\frac{8}{3} \times \frac{5}{2} =$        $\frac{15}{4} \times \frac{7}{3} =$

## Divide. Write each quotient in simplest form.

3.    $\frac{5}{6} \div \frac{5}{9} =$        $\frac{3}{8} \div \frac{3}{4} =$        $\frac{3}{4} \div \frac{5}{2} =$        $\frac{4}{5} \div \frac{4}{3} =$

4.    $\frac{5}{8} \div \frac{1}{8} =$        $\frac{4}{7} \div \frac{2}{7} =$        $\frac{5}{8} \div \frac{3}{4} =$        $\frac{2}{5} \div \frac{4}{6} =$

5.    $\frac{5}{4} \div \frac{1}{2} =$        $\frac{7}{8} \div \frac{3}{5} =$        $\frac{7}{9} \div \frac{2}{3} =$        $\frac{4}{7} \div \frac{1}{2} =$

6.    $\frac{11}{6} \div \frac{5}{2} =$      $\frac{3}{14} \div \frac{6}{7} =$      $\frac{7}{6} \div \frac{7}{8} =$       $\frac{2}{3} \div \frac{3}{7} =$

7.    $\frac{14}{3} \div \frac{4}{21} =$      $\frac{9}{10} \div \frac{1}{5} =$      $\frac{7}{8} \div \frac{21}{40} =$     $\frac{4}{3} \div \frac{2}{5} =$

# Dividing Fractions and Whole Numbers

When dividing fractions and whole numbers, first rename the whole number as a fraction with a denominator of 1.

## Examples

To divide a fraction by a whole number:

Divide $\frac{4}{5} \div 8$

$\frac{4}{5} \div 8 = \frac{4}{5} \div \frac{8}{1}$    Write whole number as a fraction with a denominator of 1.

$= \frac{4}{5} \times \frac{1}{8}$    Multiply $\frac{4}{5}$ by the reciprocal of $\frac{8}{1}$.

$= \frac{4 \times 1}{5 \times 8}$

$= \frac{4}{40}$

$= \frac{1}{10}$    Reduce answer to lowest terms.

To divide a whole number by a fraction:

Divide $5 \div \frac{3}{4}$

$5 \div \frac{3}{4} = \frac{5}{1} \div \frac{3}{4}$    Write whole number as a fraction with a denominator of 1.

$= \frac{5}{1} \times \frac{4}{3}$    Multiply $\frac{5}{1}$ by the reciprocal of $\frac{3}{4}$.

$= \frac{5 \times 4}{1 \times 3}$

$= \frac{20}{3}$

$= 6\frac{2}{3}$    Change improper fractions to mixed numbers.

## Divide. Write each quotient in simplest form.

1.     $6 \div \frac{4}{9} =$       $5 \div \frac{1}{7} =$       $\frac{4}{7} \div 8 =$       $\frac{6}{5} \div 2 =$

2.     $\frac{3}{5} \div 4 =$       $\frac{5}{8} \div 5 =$       $\frac{9}{10} \div 4 =$       $\frac{1}{6} \div 3 =$

3.     $\frac{9}{4} \div 6 =$       $\frac{5}{3} \div 4 =$       $\frac{4}{3} \div 5 =$       $\frac{8}{5} \div 5 =$

4.     $\frac{10}{9} \div 4 =$       $\frac{7}{4} \div 3 =$       $8 \div \frac{2}{3} =$       $10 \div \frac{4}{5} =$

    www.summerbridgeactivities.com     Math Connection—Grade 6—RBP0180

# Dividing Mixed Numbers

To divide mixed numbers, first write each mixed number as a fraction.

## Example

To divide a mixed number by another mixed number:

Divide $3\frac{4}{5} \div 2\frac{3}{4}$

$$3\frac{4}{5} \div 2\frac{3}{4} = \frac{19}{5} \div \frac{11}{4}$$   Write each mixed number as a an improper fraction.

$$= \frac{19}{5} \times \frac{4}{11}$$   Multiply the first fraction by the reciprocal of $\frac{11}{4}$.

$$= \frac{19 \times 4}{5 \times 11}$$

$$= \frac{76}{55}$$

$$= 1\frac{21}{55}$$   Change improper fractions to mixed numbers.
Write in simplest form if needed.

## Divide. Write each quotient in simplest form.

1.  $11\frac{1}{2} \div 2\frac{7}{8} =$    $3\frac{1}{2} \div 2 =$    $4\frac{1}{4} \div 3\frac{1}{8} =$    $3\frac{1}{2} \div 2 =$

2.  $3\frac{3}{4} \div 5 =$    $3\frac{1}{2} \div 1\frac{3}{4} =$    $6\frac{1}{3} \div 2 =$    $4\frac{5}{7} \div 3\frac{2}{3} =$

3.  $8 \div 1\frac{1}{5} =$    $12\frac{3}{8} \div 2\frac{3}{4} =$    $5\frac{3}{5} \div 4\frac{2}{3} =$    $2\frac{7}{8} \div 3\frac{1}{4} =$

4.  $9 \div 2\frac{5}{8} =$    $7\frac{1}{2} \div 2\frac{1}{2} =$    $1\frac{1}{4} \div 2\frac{1}{2} =$    $4\frac{1}{2} \div 1\frac{1}{3} =$

5.  $7 \div 3\frac{1}{2} =$    $7 \div 2\frac{1}{3} =$    $4\frac{1}{6} \div 5 =$    $2\frac{3}{4} \div 5\frac{2}{3} =$

6.  $4\frac{7}{8} \div 6\frac{1}{4} =$    $4\frac{3}{8} \div 4 =$    $10\frac{1}{2} \div 2\frac{1}{4} =$    $6\frac{2}{3} \div 5\frac{1}{3} =$

# Solving Equations with Fractions

Solve: $n \times 2\frac{2}{5} = \frac{3}{4}$

| **Step 1** | **Step 2** | **Step 3** |
|---|---|---|
| Rewrite $2\frac{2}{5}$ as an improper fraction. | Multiply both sides of the equation by the reciprocal of $\frac{12}{5}$, which is $\frac{5}{12}$. | Simplify. |
| $n \times 2\frac{2}{5} = \frac{3}{4}$ | $n \times \frac{12}{5} \times \frac{5}{12} = \frac{3}{4} \times \frac{5}{12}$ | $n \times 1 = \frac{3}{4} \times \frac{5}{12}$ |
| $n \times \frac{12}{5} = \frac{3}{4}$ | $n \times 1 = \frac{3}{4} \times \frac{5}{12}$ | $n = \frac{3}{4} \times \frac{5}{12}$ |
| | | $n = \frac{15}{48}$ |
| | | $n = \frac{5}{16}$ |

## Solve for *n*.

**1.** $n \times \frac{3}{4} = \frac{6}{20}$    $n \times \frac{3}{8} = \frac{2}{8}$    $n \times \frac{3}{10} = \frac{2}{3}$

**2.** $n \times \frac{1}{2} = \frac{1}{2}$    $n \times \frac{5}{6} = \frac{1}{3}$    $n \times \frac{3}{6} = 1\frac{1}{8}$

**3.** $n \times \frac{3}{8} = \frac{1}{8}$    $n \times 1\frac{1}{3} = 3$    $n \times 1\frac{1}{2} = 20$

**4.** $n \times 1\frac{1}{2} = 3\frac{1}{2}$    $n \times \frac{1}{8} = \frac{2}{3}$    $n \times \frac{2}{3} = 14$

**5.** $n \times \frac{1}{7} = 5\frac{1}{4}$    $n \times \frac{4}{5} = 20$    $n \times 2\frac{3}{4} = 16\frac{1}{2}$

**Ask Yourself:**
• Did I rewrite mixed numbers as improper fractions?
• Did I multiply both sides of the equation by the <u>reciprocal</u>?

# Solving Equations with Fractions

Solve: $n \div \frac{3}{4} = \frac{5}{6}$

| **Step 1** | **Step 2** | **Step 3** |
|---|---|---|
| Divide $n$ by $\frac{3}{4}$. So, multiply by the reciprocal. | Multiply both sides of the equation by the reciprocal of $\frac{4}{3}$, which is $\frac{3}{4}$. | Simplify. |
| $n \div \frac{3}{4} = \frac{5}{6}$ | $n \times \frac{4}{3} \times \frac{3}{4} = \frac{5}{6} \times \frac{3}{4}$ | $n \times 1 = \frac{5}{6} \times \frac{3}{4}$ |
| $n \times \frac{4}{3} = \frac{5}{6}$ | $n \times 1 = \frac{5}{6} \times \frac{3}{4}$ | $n = \frac{5}{6} \times \frac{3}{4}$ |
| | | $n = \frac{15}{24}$ |
| | | $n = \frac{5}{8}$ |

## Solve for $n$.

1.  $n \div \frac{1}{2} = \frac{7}{10}$  $\qquad$  $n \div \frac{5}{6} = 10$  $\qquad$  $n \div \frac{3}{4} = 3\frac{1}{2}$

2.  $n \div \frac{2}{9} = \frac{1}{5}$  $\qquad$  $n \div \frac{3}{10} = 12$  $\qquad$  $n \div \frac{1}{3} = 1\frac{1}{4}$

3.  $n \div \frac{1}{12} = \frac{1}{2}$  $\qquad$  $n \div \frac{3}{8} = \frac{1}{2}$  $\qquad$  $n \div \frac{3}{4} = 16$

4.  $n \div 4\frac{2}{3} = 1$  $\qquad$  $n \div 2\frac{4}{9} = 6$  $\qquad$  $n \div 1\frac{5}{7} = 5$

5.  $n \div 3\frac{1}{3} = 5\frac{5}{8}$  $\qquad$  $n \div 1\frac{3}{4} = 1\frac{1}{2}$  $\qquad$  $n \div 5\frac{1}{4} = 2\frac{1}{2}$

**Remember:**
Rewrite all mixed numbers and whole numbers as fractions before solving the equation.

## Downhill Division Practice

Start at the top of the hill. Follow the skier by filling in the blanks as you divide your way down the hill. Can you get the final answer?

Hint:  If you get stuck, try working backwards by multiplying!!

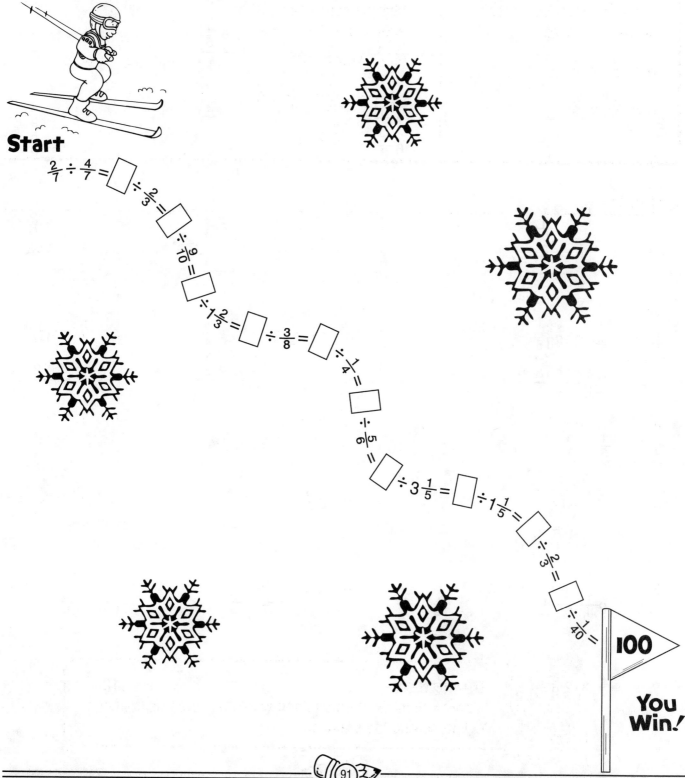

**Start**

$$\frac{2}{7} \div \frac{4}{7} = \boxed{\phantom{0}}$$

$$\div \frac{2}{3} = \boxed{\phantom{0}}$$

$$\div \frac{9}{10} = \boxed{\phantom{0}}$$

$$\div 1\frac{2}{3} = \boxed{\phantom{0}} \div \frac{3}{8} = \boxed{\phantom{0}} \div \frac{1}{4} = \boxed{\phantom{0}}$$

$$\div \frac{5}{6} = \boxed{\phantom{0}} \div 3\frac{1}{5} = \boxed{\phantom{0}} \div 1\frac{1}{5} = \boxed{\phantom{0}}$$

$$\div \frac{2}{3} = \boxed{\phantom{0}}$$

$$\div \frac{1}{40} = \boxed{100}$$

**You Win!**

© RBP Books          www.summerbridgeactivities.com                    Math Connection—Grade 6—RBP0180

# Operation Fraction Action

Here is a chance to practice your fraction skills.

## Write each answer as a fraction or a mixed number in simplest form.

1.
$$\begin{array}{r} \frac{4}{8} \\ + \frac{1}{3} \\ \hline \end{array}$$
$$\begin{array}{r} \frac{1}{2} \\ + \frac{6}{12} \\ \hline \end{array}$$
$$\begin{array}{r} 2\frac{2}{3} \\ + 3\frac{4}{5} \\ \hline \end{array}$$
$$\begin{array}{r} \frac{5}{6} \\ + \frac{1}{2} \\ \hline \end{array}$$

2.
$$\begin{array}{r} \frac{2}{5} \\ + \frac{4}{15} \\ \hline \end{array}$$
$$\begin{array}{r} 3\frac{3}{4} \\ + 6\frac{1}{3} \\ \hline \end{array}$$
$$\begin{array}{r} \frac{4}{6} \\ - \frac{2}{6} \\ \hline \end{array}$$
$$\begin{array}{r} \frac{8}{9} \\ - \frac{5}{9} \\ \hline \end{array}$$

3.
$$\begin{array}{r} \frac{4}{5} \\ - \frac{2}{3} \\ \hline \end{array}$$
$$\begin{array}{r} \frac{3}{4} \\ - \frac{3}{6} \\ \hline \end{array}$$
$$\begin{array}{r} 9\frac{2}{3} \\ - 4\frac{7}{8} \\ \hline \end{array}$$
$$\begin{array}{r} 7\frac{2}{5} \\ - 4\frac{2}{3} \\ \hline \end{array}$$

4.
$$\begin{array}{r} 2\frac{4}{18} \\ - 2\frac{3}{18} \\ \hline \end{array}$$
$$\begin{array}{r} 3\frac{4}{5} \\ + 10\frac{1}{2} \\ \hline \end{array}$$
$$\begin{array}{r} 6\frac{3}{4} \\ - 3\frac{1}{2} \\ \hline \end{array}$$
$$\begin{array}{r} 1\frac{5}{8} \\ + 2\frac{7}{24} \\ \hline \end{array}$$

5. $\frac{1}{5} \times \frac{3}{7} =$    $2\frac{2}{5} \times 10 =$    $1\frac{1}{6} \times 3\frac{3}{8} =$    $3\frac{2}{5} \times \frac{1}{6} =$

6. $7 \div \frac{1}{4} =$    $1\frac{3}{8} \div \frac{2}{4} =$    $\frac{2}{5} \div 8 =$    $\frac{1}{3} \div 2\frac{3}{4} =$

7. $2\frac{1}{4} \times 1\frac{7}{12} =$    $\frac{6}{10} \div \frac{1}{5} =$    $2\frac{2}{7} \times \frac{6}{9} =$    $2\frac{2}{9} \div \frac{5}{8} =$

8. $\frac{4}{7} \times 2\frac{8}{9} =$    $\frac{6}{13} \times \frac{2}{3} =$    $3\frac{1}{3} \div \frac{4}{9} =$    $12 \div 2\frac{7}{8} =$

92

# Food Fractions: Problem Solving

## Solve each problem.

1. A box contains 10 ounces of cereal. If one serving is $1\frac{1}{4}$ ounces, how many servings are in the box?

   There are ____ servings in the cereal box.

2. A can of soup contains $22\frac{3}{4}$ ounces. If one can contains $3\frac{1}{2}$ servings of soup, how many ounces are in one serving?

   There are ____ ounces of soup in one serving.

3. Ten melons weigh $17\frac{1}{2}$ pounds. What is the average weight of each melon?

   The average weight of each melon is ____ pounds.

4. Christine bought $\frac{3}{4}$ pounds of grapes to put in her sack lunches. If she eats the same amount each day for 5 days, how much does she eat each day?

   She eats ____ ounces of grapes each day.

5. Mrs. Wilson bought $5\frac{1}{2}$ feet of licorice to share equally with her five children and herself. How many feet of licorice will each person receive? How many inches of licorice will each person receive?

   **Think:**
   How many inches are in a foot?

   Each person will receive ____ feet or ____ inches of licorice.

6. Mrs. Wilson bought a 35-ounce package of flour. She used $\frac{1}{3}$ of it to bake 5 loaves of bread. How many ounces of flour were in each loaf of bread?

   **Clue:**
   Solve a simpler problem. How much of the flour did she use?

   There are ____ ounces of flour in each loaf of bread.

7. Mrs. Wilson bought a $2\frac{3}{4}$ pound roast for their family dinner. A total of 9 people will be at the dinner. How many ounces of roast will each person get if the roast is divided up equally?

   Each person will get ____ ounces of roast.

www.summerbridgeactivities.com

# Planetary Weights: Problem Solving

An object on another planet or on the moon will weigh a fractional part of its Earth weight. The following chart shows the fractional part of an object's Earth weight on some other planets and on the moon.

| Saturn | Mars | Venus | Earth's Moon |
|--------|------|-------|--------------|
| $1\frac{1}{5}$ | $\frac{19}{50}$ | $\frac{5}{6}$ | $\frac{1}{6}$ |

Multiply to find an object's weight on another planet when you know its Earth weight.

Kevin weighs 165 pounds on Earth. How much would Kevin weigh on Venus?

$$\frac{165}{1} \times \frac{5}{6} = 137\frac{1}{2} \text{ pounds}$$

Kevin would weigh $137\frac{1}{2}$ pounds on Venus.

Divide to find an object's weight on Earth when you know its weight on another planet.

A boulder weighs 950 pounds on Mars. How much would the boulder weigh on Earth?

$$\frac{950}{1} \div \frac{19}{50} = 2,500 \text{ pounds}$$

The boulder would weigh 2,500 pounds on Earth.

## Find each answer.

1. How much would Kevin weigh on Saturn if he weighs 165 pounds on Earth?

2. An astronaut collected some moon rocks that weighed $12\frac{3}{5}$ pounds on the moon. How much did these moon rocks weigh on Earth?

3. An astronaut and all his gear weigh 220 pounds on Earth. How much would the astronaut weigh on Venus?

4. If a meteorite weighs $28\frac{1}{2}$ pounds on Mars, how much will it weigh on Earth?

5. Some dirt samples are estimated to weigh $21\frac{3}{4}$ pounds on Saturn. How much do these dirt samples weigh on Earth?

6. If an astronaut's life-support system weighs 25 pounds on the moon, how much would it weigh on Mars?

# Post-Test: Dividing Fractions

## Write the reciprocal of the number.

1. $\dfrac{3}{4}$ $\qquad$ $\dfrac{8}{5}$ $\qquad$ $5\dfrac{1}{3}$ $\qquad$ $7$ $\qquad$ $10\dfrac{1}{5}$

## Divide. Write each fraction or mixed number in simplest form.

2. $4 \div \dfrac{1}{2} =$ $\qquad$ $2 \div \dfrac{1}{10} =$ $\qquad$ $3 \div \dfrac{3}{6} =$ $\qquad$ $4 \div \dfrac{4}{6} =$

3. $7 \div \dfrac{2}{3} =$ $\qquad$ $\dfrac{1}{3} \div \dfrac{1}{9} =$ $\qquad$ $\dfrac{3}{6} \div \dfrac{1}{2} =$ $\qquad$ $\dfrac{1}{6} \div \dfrac{2}{6} =$

4. $\dfrac{2}{3} \div \dfrac{4}{5} =$ $\qquad$ $\dfrac{5}{8} \div \dfrac{3}{6} =$ $\qquad$ $4\dfrac{1}{2} \div \dfrac{1}{3} =$ $\qquad$ $2\dfrac{2}{5} \div \dfrac{2}{3} =$

5. $\dfrac{3}{4} \div 4 =$ $\qquad$ $1\dfrac{1}{6} \div 3 =$ $\qquad$ $3\dfrac{3}{5} \div 2 =$ $\qquad$ $2 \div 2\dfrac{1}{2} =$

6. $\dfrac{6}{4} \div 1\dfrac{3}{8} =$ $\qquad$ $1\dfrac{3}{4} \div 2\dfrac{4}{6} =$ $\qquad$ $\dfrac{8}{5} \div 2\dfrac{2}{5} =$ $\qquad$ $2\dfrac{3}{5} \div 1\dfrac{3}{9} =$

## Solve the equations for *n*.

7. $n \times \dfrac{5}{7} = \dfrac{3}{10}$ $\qquad\qquad\qquad\qquad$ $n \div \dfrac{1}{7} = \dfrac{1}{5}$

8. $n \times 1\dfrac{1}{4} = 3\dfrac{5}{8}$ $\qquad\qquad\qquad\qquad$ $n \div 3\dfrac{4}{9} = 2\dfrac{2}{3}$

## Solve the problem.

9. Dennis wants to form a team to run a relay race. Each team member will need to run $\dfrac{5}{8}$ mile. The whole race is $3\dfrac{3}{4}$ miles. How many relay runners does Dennis need on his team?

www.summerbridgeactivities.com $\qquad$ Math Connection—Grade 6—RBP0180

# Geometry: Plane Figures

A **point** is a location in space. **Space** is the set of all points.

A **plane** is a set of flat points that form a flat surface extending in all directions without limit.

Here are some figures that are contained in a plane:

| Segment | Ray | Line |
|---|---|---|
| The endpoints of this segment are **A** and **B**. | A ray has one endpoint and extends forever in the other direction. | The arrowheads show that a line extends forever in both directions. |

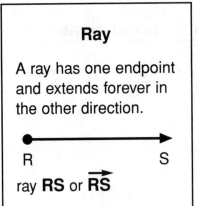

Segment **AB** or $\overline{AB}$

segment **BA** or $\overline{BA}$

ray **RS** or $\overrightarrow{RS}$

line **CD** or $\overleftrightarrow{CD}$

line **DC** or $\overleftrightarrow{DC}$

## Write the name or names for each figure as shown. Use correct symbols.

1.

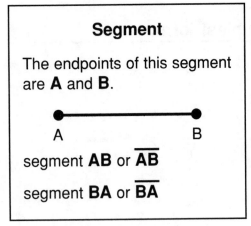
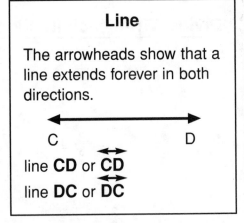

$\overleftrightarrow{CD}$ or $\overleftrightarrow{DC}$            _____         _____ or _____     _____ or _____

2.

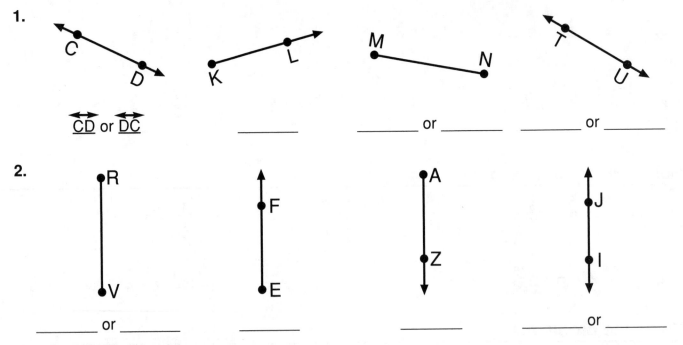

_____ or _____       _____         _____         _____ or _____

## Draw an example of each figure.

3.        line XY               segment PQ           ray GH              line YZ

# Geometry: Classifying Lines

If lines cross through the same point, they **intersect**. If they intersect at right angles, they are **perpendicular**. If they do not intersect, no matter how far they extend, they are **parallel**.

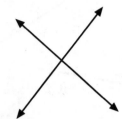

The lines intersect.

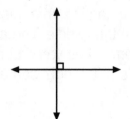

The lines are perpendicular.

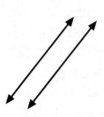

The lines are parallel.

Rays and segments can also intersect, or be perpendicular or parallel.

## Match the term with the correct figure.

1. ____    intersecting rays                              A.

2. ____    parallel segments                              B.

3. ____    perpendicular line and ray                     C.

4. ____    intersecting segment and line                  D.

5. ____    perpendicular lines                            E.

6. ____    parallel ray and segment                       F.

7. ____    parallel line and ray                          G.

8. ____    segments intersecting at point P               H.

9. ____    perpendicular segment and ray                  I.
           intersecting at endpoint S

# Geometry: Classifying Angles

Two rays that share a common endpoint form an **angle**. The common endpoint is the **vertex** of the angle. The two rays are the **sides** of the angle.

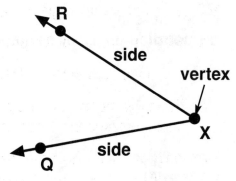

The symbol ∠ represents an angle. In naming an angle, make sure the letter that names the vertex is in the middle. The angle at the right is ∠**QXR** or ∠**RXQ**. Sometimes you can name an angle using only the vertex. The angle at the right can also be called ∠**X**.

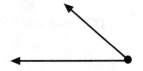

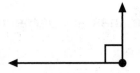

| An **acute angle** is smaller than a right angle. | A **right angle** is like the corner of an index card. | An **obtuse angle** is greater than a right angle, but not a straight line. |

## Example:

Name the angle to the right three ways. Classify as acute, right, obtuse, or straight. The vertex is S. The angle can be named ∠**UST**, ∠**TSU**, or ∠**S**. Because the angle is smaller than a right angle, it is **acute**.

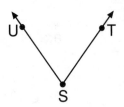

## Name each angle three ways. Classify the angle as acute, right, or obtuse.

**1.**

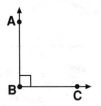   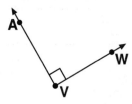

_____ _____ _____ _____

**2.**

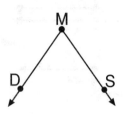 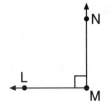 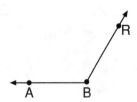 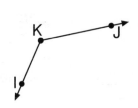

_____ _____ _____ _____

# Geometry: Measuring Angles

You can measure an angle using an instrument called a protractor. To measure ∠**ABC**:

1. Place the center of the protractor at **B**, the vertex of the angle.

2. Place the zero mark on **BC**, one side of the angle.

3. Read the measure of the angle where **BA**, the other side of the angle, crosses the protractor. The measure of ∠**ABC** is **70°**.

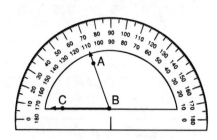

**Remember:** Classify angles by their measurement.
**right angle** → measures exactly **90°**
**acute angle** → measures less than **90°**
**obtuse angle** → measures greater than **90°**, but less than **180°**

## Use a protractor to measure each angle.

Then write the measurement and classify the angle as acute, right, or obtuse.

**1.**

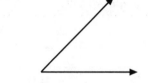   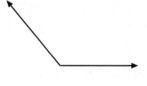   

_____   _____   _____

**2.**

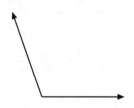   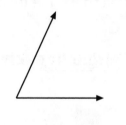   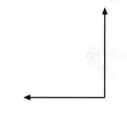

_____   _____   _____

**3.**

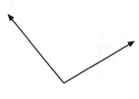   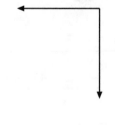   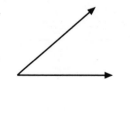

_____   _____   _____

**4.**

   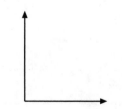   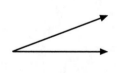

_____   _____   _____

www.summerbridgeactivities.com   **Math Connection—Grade 6—RBP0180**

# Geometry: Classifying Triangles by Their Angles

A **triangle** is a closed figure made from three line segments. The sum of the angles in any triangle always equals **180°**.

Triangles can be classified by the size of their angles.

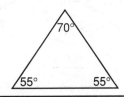

| An **acute triangle** has three acute angles. |
|:---:|

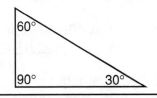

| A **right triangle** has exactly one right angle. |
|:---:|

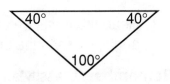

| An **obtuse triangle** has exactly one obtuse angle. |
|:---:|

## Example:

Find the measure of the missing angle in the triangle.
Classify as acute, right, or obtuse.

**Remember: The sum of the angles will add up to 180°.**
  Write the equation using the given measures. $n + 35 + 60 = 180$
  Add the given measures. $35 + 60 = 95$
  Solve the equation. $180 - 95 = 85$

So, the missing angle measure is **85°**.

All three angles of the triangle are less than 90°, so the triangle is **acute**.

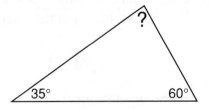

$$35 + 60 + ? = 180$$
$$95 + ? = 180$$
$$95 + 85 = 180$$

## Find the measure of the missing angle in each triangle.

Classify the triangle as acute, right, or obtuse.

**1.**

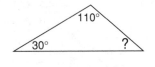

**40°**

**acute**

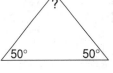

_____

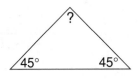

_____

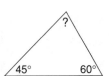

_____

**2.**

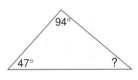

_____
_____

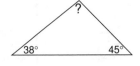

_____
_____

_____
_____

_____
_____

Math Connection—Grade 6—RBP0180          www.summerbridgeactivities.com          ©RBP Books

# Functions and Patterns

The figures below are models of buildings made with "blocks." Notice the pattern that relates the number of blocks in the tower and the total number of blocks used in the building.

The building with 1 block
for its tower takes 6 blocks
to build.

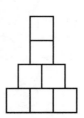

The building with 2 blocks
for its tower takes 7 blocks
to build.

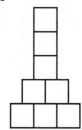

The building with 3 blocks
for its tower takes 8 blocks
to build.

How many blocks in the building with 4 cubes for its tower? _____

How many blocks in the building with 10 cubes for its tower? _____

How many blocks in the building with 20 cubes for its tower? _____

Look at the table and the statement that gives the general rule for the pattern.

| Number of Blocks in Tower | 1 | 2 | 3 | 4 | 10 | 20 |
|---|---|---|---|---|---|---|
| Number of Blocks in Entire Building | 6 | 7 | 8 | 9 | 15 | 25 |

**Think:** The difference is…        +5        +5        +5        +5        +5        +5

To find the number of blocks in a building, __**add five**__ to the number of blocks in the tower.

## Complete each table. Then fill in the statement that gives the general rule for the pattern.

1.

The kite with
**1 tile** for its
tail takes **10**
tiles to make.

The kite with
**2 tiles** for its
tail takes **11**
tiles to make.

The kite with
**3 tiles** for its
tail takes **12**
tiles to make.

| Number of Tiles in Tail | 1 | 2 | 3 | 4 | 10 | 20 |
|---|---|---|---|---|---|---|
| Number of Tiles in Entire Kite | 10 | 11 | 12 | | | |

To find the number of tiles in the kite, _____ to the number of tiles in the tail.

## Functions and Patterns

**1.**

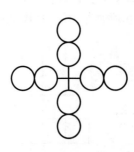

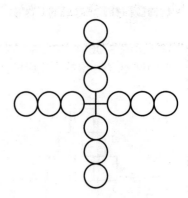

The design with **1** circle extending on each branch is made with a total of **4** circles.

The design with **2** circles extending on each branch is made with a total of **8** circles.

The design with **3** circles extending on each branch is made with a total of **12** circles.

| Number of Circles in Each Branch | 1 | 2 | 3 | 4 | 10 | 20 |
|---|---|---|---|---|---|---|
| Number of Circles in Entire Design | 4 | 8 | 12 | | | |

To find the number of circles in the design, _____ the number of circles on each branch by _____.

**2.**

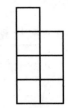

The "chair" **2** blocks tall takes **3** blocks to build.

The "chair" **3** blocks tall takes **5** blocks to build.

The "chair" **4** blocks tall takes **7** blocks to build.

| Height of Chair in Blocks | 2 | 3 | 4 | 5 | 6 | 10 | 100 |
|---|---|---|---|---|---|---|---|
| Number of Blocks in Entire Chair | 3 | 5 | 7 | | | | |

To find the number of blocks in a chair, multiply the number of blocks in the chair's height by _____ and subtract _____.

Math Connection—Grade 6—RBP0180        www.summerbridgeactivities.com        ©RBP Books

# Number Patterns: Tables

Write a method for calculating *y* if you know *x*. Then complete the table.

| x | y |
|---|---|
| 0 | 2 |
| 1 | 3 |
| 2 | 4 |
| 3 | 5 |
| 4 | **6** |
| 8 | **10** |

To get from 0 to 2, **add 2**.
To get from 1 to 3, **add 2**.
To get from 2 to 4, **add 2**.
To get from 3 to 5, **add 2**.

The rule is:  Add **x** and **2**, or **y = x + 2**.
For x = 4,  y = 4 + 2 = **6**
For x = 8,  y = 8 + 2 = **10**

In the table to the right, *y* is 2 times *x*.
So the rule for finding *y* is to multiply *x* by 2.

| x | 0 | 1 | 2 | 3 |
|---|---|---|---|---|
| y | 0 | 2 | 4 | 6 |

## Find the rule for calculating *y*. Then complete each table.

**1.**

| x | 1 | 3 | 5 | 7 | 9 | 11 |
|---|---|---|---|---|---|----|
| y | 5 | 7 | 9 |   |   |    |

Rule: _____

| x | 6 | 7 | 8 | 9 | 10 | 11 |
|---|---|---|---|---|----|----|
| y | 4 | 5 | 6 |   |    |    |

Rule: _____

**2.**

| x | 3  | 4  | 5  | 6 | 7 | 8 |
|---|----|----|----|---|---|---|
| y | 12 | 16 | 20 |   |   |   |

Rule: _____

| x | 2 | 4  | 6  | 8 | 10 | 12 |
|---|---|----|----|---|----|----|
| y | 6 | 12 | 18 |   |    |    |

Rule: _____

**3.**

| x | 6 | 8 | 10 | 12 | 14 | 16 |
|---|---|---|----|----|----|----|
| y | 3 | 4 | 5  |    |    |    |

Rule: _____

| x | 3 | 7 | 8 | 5 | 10 | 21 |
|---|---|---|---|---|----|----|
| y | 2 | 6 | 7 |   |    |    |

Rule: _____

**4.**

| x | 2  | 3  | 4  | 5 | 6 | 7 |
|---|----|----|----|---|---|---|
| y | 17 | 18 | 19 |   |   |   |

Rule: _____

| x | 10 | 11 | 12 | 13 | 14 | 15 |
|---|----|----|----|----|----|----|
| y | 20 | 22 | 24 |    |    |    |

Rule: _____

www.summerbridgeactivities.com          Math Connection—Grade 6—RBP0180

# Statistics and Probability
Using Mean, Median, Mode, and Range to Summarize Data

What does it mean when you hear, "The runners averaged **4** miles each day?"

Find the range, mean, median, and mode of this data set.

| | |
|---|---|
| Distances covered by Run-for-Your-Life participants: 5 miles, 8 miles, 3 miles, 1 mile, 3 miles. | The **mean** (or **average**): The sum of the items divided by the number of items. $$\frac{5+8+3+1+3}{5} = \frac{20}{5} \text{ or } \textbf{4 miles}$$ |

The **range**: The difference between the greatest value (**8**) and the least value (**1**) in the data.
$$8 - 1 = \textbf{7 miles}$$

The **mode**: The number that occurs most frequently.

$$1 \quad 3 \quad 3 \quad 5 \quad 8$$
**mode**

A data set can have more than one mode. For example **1, 3, 3, 5, 8, 8**, has two modes: **3** and **8**. If no number occurs more frequently than the others, the data have no mode.

The **median**: The middle number when the data are arranged from least to greatest.

$$1 \quad 3 \quad 3 \quad 5 \quad 8$$
↑
**median**

If there are two middle numbers, use the average of the two.

## Find the mean, median, mode, and range of the set of data.

**1.**   34, 41, 33, 41, 31

Mean _____    Median _____

Mode _____    Range _____

18, 12, 10, 8, 14, 35, 10, 21

Mean _____    Median _____

Mode _____    Range _____

**2.**   $7, $10, $14, $23, $16

Mean _____    Median _____

Mode _____    Range _____

$41, $18, $63, $24, $41, $72, $84

Mean _____    Median _____

Mode _____    Range _____

**3.** The data show the number of points scored by the Shooting Stars basketball team in their last 12 games. Find the mean, median, mode, and range of the data.

87, 112, 98, 93, 79, 80, 89, 83, 91, 93, 86, 101

Mean _____    Median _____    Mode _____    Range _____

# Statistics and Probability
Making Predictions from Samples

A **sample** is a small set or group taken from a large set or population group. **Predictions** can be made about the large group by looking at the results of the sample group.

## Example:
Cody has a box with **200** marbles in it. The marbles are red, green, yellow, and blue. Without looking, Cody took a random sample of **20** marbles out of the box. In this sample, **8** of the marbles were red. How many red marbles should Cody predict are in the box?

**Step 1**     Write a proportion in the form of equivalent fractions.

red marbles in sample   →     $\dfrac{8}{20} = \dfrac{n}{200}$     → red marbles in box
total marbles in sample →                                              → total marbles in box

**Step 2**     Use equivalent fractions to solve.

$\dfrac{8 \times 10}{20 \times 10} = \dfrac{80}{200}$     So, Cody should predict there are **80** red marbles in the box of 200 marbles.

## Solve.

1. In a sample, 11 out of 25 marbles are green. Predict how many green marbles are in a box of 100 marbles.

2. In a sample, 54 out of 75 middle school students said they planned to go to the school carnival. Based on this sample, how many of the 750 middle school students would you predict will go to the carnival?

3. In a sample of sixth graders, 50 students were asked if they would enter a writing contest. Of that number, 32 said "yes," they would enter the contest. Based on this sample, how many of the 250 sixth graders will enter the writing contest?

4. A representative sample of T-shirt sizes of 25 sixth graders was taken. The results were Small: 3, Medium: 9, Large: 13. How many of each size should be ordered for 250 students in the sixth grade?

5. A sample of 50 sixth graders were asked which of the 4 candidates they planned to vote for in the election for class president. Janet Garcia had the greatest support with 13 students planning to vote for her. Based on this sample, how many sixth grade votes can Janet count on for the election if there are 300 sixth graders voting?

# Fractions to Decimals

Using equivalent fractions to write fractions as decimals.

For my next trick, I'll change this fraction into a decimal.

## Examples:

Solve:

Write $\frac{1}{5}$ as a decimal in tenths.

Rewrite $\frac{1}{5}$ as a fraction with a denominator of 10.

$$\frac{1 \times 2}{5 \times 2} = \frac{2}{10} = .2$$

Solve:

Write $\frac{3}{4}$ as a decimal in hundredths.

Rewrite $\frac{3}{4}$ as a fraction with a denominator of 100.

$$\frac{3 \times 25}{4 \times 25} = \frac{75}{100} = .75$$

Solve:

Write $2\frac{14}{125}$ as a decimal in thousandths.

Rewrite $2\frac{14}{125}$ as a whole number plus a fraction with a denominator of 1000.

$$2 + \frac{14 \times 8}{125 \times 8} = 2 + \frac{112}{1000} = 2\frac{112}{1000} = 2.112$$

## Write each fraction or mixed number as a decimal in tenths.

1.  $\frac{1}{2}$      $\frac{2}{5}$      $\frac{3}{10}$      $3\frac{4}{5}$      $4\frac{6}{10}$

## Write each fraction or mixed number as a decimal in hundredths.

2.  $\frac{2}{4}$      $1\frac{1}{10}$      $\frac{9}{25}$      $3\frac{16}{50}$      $\frac{3}{5}$

3.  $4\frac{7}{20}$      $\frac{1}{2}$      $2\frac{8}{100}$      $\frac{4}{10}$      $\frac{24}{25}$

4.  $\frac{1}{4}$      $6\frac{15}{20}$      $\frac{4}{5}$      $7\frac{5}{100}$      $\frac{26}{50}$

## Write each fraction or mixed number as a decimal in thousandths.

5.  $\frac{3}{8}$      $\frac{1}{5}$      $5\frac{12}{25}$      $\frac{25}{40}$      $3\frac{7}{100}$

6.  $\frac{28}{500}$      $1\frac{3}{250}$      $\frac{1}{4}$      $8\frac{18}{50}$      $\frac{56}{125}$

7.  $6\frac{1}{2}$      $\frac{789}{1000}$      $4\frac{40}{250}$      $\frac{2}{125}$      $2\frac{5}{8}$

Math Connection—Grade 6—RBP0180      www.summerbridgeactivities.com      © RBP Books

# Decimals to Fractions

**Examples:**

Write each decimal as a fraction or mixed number in simplest form.

$0.15 = \frac{15}{100}$

Reduce to lowest terms $\rightarrow \frac{15}{100} = \frac{3}{20}$

$5.6 = 5\frac{6}{10}$

$5\frac{6}{10} = 5\frac{3}{5}$

$0.064 = \frac{64}{1000}$

$\frac{64}{1000} = \frac{8}{125}$

## Write each decimal as a fraction or mixed number in simplest form.

| | | | |
|---|---|---|---|
| **1.** 0.1 | 2.6 | 0.4 | 6.5 |
| **2.** 8.7 | 0.9 | 4.8 | 0.3 |
| **3.** 0.20 | 0.25 | 0.55 | 6.34 |
| **4.** 8.08 | 0.04 | 0.01 | 4.06 |
| **5.** 0.42 | 1.75 | 0.488 | 0.86 |
| **6.** 2.500 | 0.505 | 3.404 | 0.532 |
| **7.** 7.266 | 0.275 | 9.454 | 0.844 |
| **8.** 0.005 | .020 | 3.900 | 0.008 |

# Pre-Test: Adding and Subtracting Decimals

## Add or subtract.

**1.**
|  | 21.2 |
| --- | --- |
| 0.1 | 8.406 |
| + 0.08 | + 40.120 |

6.304
+ 2.180

**2.**
|  |  |  |
| --- | --- | --- |
| 0.26 | 6.461 | 18.269 |
| − 0.03 | − 0.350 | − 3.108 |

**3.**
|  |  | 14.16 |
| --- | --- | --- |
| 0.48 | 6.783 | 9.84 |
| + 0.7 | + 9.4 | + 6.408 |

**4.**
|  |  |  |
| --- | --- | --- |
| 0.206 | 6.03 | 24.4 |
| − 0.18 | − 4.169 | − 8.627 |

## Solve each problem.

**5.** Cole used his credit card to purchase $115.67 worth of clothing at the department store. The next day, he returned a tie that cost $15.99 and a belt that cost $16.50. How much will the credit card company charge him for the clothing he kept?

**6.** Tammy swam the length of the pool in 35.6 seconds on Wednesday. This was 1.7 seconds faster than she swam it on Tuesday. What was her time on Tuesday?

# Adding and Subtracting Decimals

Adding and subtracting decimals is like adding and subtracting whole numbers.

**Step 1**
Line up the decimal points.
Add or subtract as you would with whole numbers.

**Step 2**
Write the decimal point in the answer.

Add.
**8.25 + 7.62**

$$\begin{array}{r} 8.25 \\ + 7.62 \\ \hline 15\ 87 \end{array}$$

$\longrightarrow$

$$\begin{array}{r} 8.25 \\ + 7.62 \\ \hline 15.87 \end{array}$$ **decimal point**

Subtract.
**17.05 − 11.51**

$$\begin{array}{r} {\scriptstyle 6\ 10} \\ 1\cancel{7}.05 \\ - 11.51 \\ \hline 5\ 54 \end{array}$$

$\longrightarrow$

$$\begin{array}{r} {\scriptstyle 6\ 10} \\ 1\cancel{7}.05 \\ - 11.51 \\ \hline 5.54 \end{array}$$ **decimal point**

## Add or subtract.

**1.**

| 7.59 | $4.88 | $25.90 | 157.8 | 83.041 |
|---|---|---|---|---|
| + 2.09 | + 6.76 | + 34.80 | + 30.1 | + 5.226 |

**2.**

| 10.42 | $52.99 | 18.45 | 14.07 | $19.99 |
|---|---|---|---|---|
| − 6.01 | − 25.00 | − 5.10 | − 2.88 | − 12.70 |

**3.**

| 3.041 | $15.08 | $35.33 | 5.001 | 145.2 |
|---|---|---|---|---|
| 5.226 | 46.09 | 19.38 | 64.893 | 452.8 |
| + 0.451 | + 145.73 | + 10.94 | + 158.116 | + 68.4 |

**4.**

| $36.05 | 6.08 | $58.00 | 19.44 | 99.421 |
|---|---|---|---|---|
| − 14.99 | − 4.18 | − 42.64 | − 11.79 | − 77.025 |

**5.**      153.71 + 1.42 =      61.108 + 6.225 =      49.22 + 5.81 + 4.85 =

**6.**      4.45 − 3.29 =      17.89 − 6.52 =      7.462 − 2.473 =

You will need to write these with the decimal points lined up.

# Adding Decimals

Sometimes it helps to write 0's to help you keep track of your place value columns.

Add    **152.6 + 0.765**

**Step 1**
Line up the decimal points.
Place a zero where it helps you add.

$$
\begin{array}{r}
152.6\mathbf{00} \\
+\ \ \ 0.765
\end{array}
$$

← Place a **0** in the hundredths and thousandths place.

**Step 2**
Add as you would with whole numbers.
Write the decimal point in the answer.

$$
\begin{array}{r}
^{1}\\
152.600 \\
+\ \ \ 0.765 \\
\hline
153.365
\end{array}
$$

↑    **Don't forget.**

## Add.

**1.**

$$
\begin{array}{r} 0.9 \\ +\ 0.47 \end{array}
\qquad
\begin{array}{r} 6 \\ +\ 7.48 \end{array}
\qquad
\begin{array}{r} 8.043 \\ +\ 3.97 \end{array}
\qquad
\begin{array}{r} 6.08 \\ +\ 48.463 \end{array}
\qquad
\begin{array}{r} 37.27 \\ +\ 84.948 \end{array}
$$

**2.**

$$
\begin{array}{r} 36.764 \\ +\ 877.3 \end{array}
\qquad
\begin{array}{r} 97.4 \\ +\ 73.969 \end{array}
\qquad
\begin{array}{r} 53.903 \\ +\ 99.8 \end{array}
\qquad
\begin{array}{r} 0.6 \\ +\ 69.427 \end{array}
\qquad
\begin{array}{r} 47.67 \\ +\ 0.4 \end{array}
$$

**3.**

$$
\begin{array}{r} 0.6 \\ 0.47 \\ +\ 0.22 \end{array}
\qquad
\begin{array}{r} 24.69 \\ 0.104 \\ +\ 682.62 \end{array}
\qquad
\begin{array}{r} 7 \\ 32.08 \\ +\ 456.643 \end{array}
\qquad
\begin{array}{r} 28.1 \\ 7.786 \\ +\ 246.907 \end{array}
\qquad
\begin{array}{r} 39.48 \\ 12.2 \\ +\ 473.745 \end{array}
$$

**4.**

$$
\begin{array}{r} 6.107 \\ 65.48 \\ +\ 183 \end{array}
\qquad
\begin{array}{r} 0.72 \\ 2.1 \\ +\ 135.461 \end{array}
\qquad
\begin{array}{r} 0.74 \\ 8 \\ +\ 10.9 \end{array}
\qquad
\begin{array}{r} 0.5 \\ 9.43 \\ +\ 0.002 \end{array}
\qquad
\begin{array}{r} 4.673 \\ 38.09 \\ +\ 196.4 \end{array}
$$

**5.**    97.483 + 73.99 =    5.903 + 99.1 =      18.7 + 6.427 =

**6.**    74.36 + 8.758 =    8.05 + 139.5 + 98.004 =    78 + 746.78 + 9.463 =

**Remember:**
Writing zeros to the right of the decimal number does not change the value of the number.

*Math Connection—Grade 6—RBP0180*           www.summerbridgeactivities.com        ©RBP Books

# Subtracting Decimals

Subtract    **48 − 5.73**

### Step 1
Line up the decimal points.
Place a zero where it helps you subtract.

48.**00**  ◄── Place a **0** in the tenths and
− 5.73            hundredths place.

### Step 2
Subtract as you would with whole numbers.
Write the decimal point in the answer.

$$
\begin{array}{r}
9 \\
7\,10\,10 \\
4\,\cancel{8}.\cancel{0}\cancel{0} \\
-\ 5.73 \\
\hline
42.27
\end{array}
$$

## Subtract.

| | | | | | |
|---|---|---|---|---|---|
| **1.** | 6.2<br>− 0.76 | 7.2<br>− 3.94 | $4<br>− 1.70 | 7<br>− 2.85 | 6<br>− 2.76 |
| **2.** | $4.54<br>− 3 | 28.4<br>− 9.63 | 437.1<br>− 67.34 | 268<br>− 168.94 | 63.4<br>− 0.099 |
| **3.** | 20.1<br>− 0.673 | 47.2<br>− 0.499 | $70.23<br>− 68 | 64.6<br>− 35.072 | $42.21<br>− 28 |
| **4.** | 167.6<br>− 87.907 | 7.2<br>− 0.093 | 4.5<br>− 2.408 | 278.905<br>− 188 | 7.2<br>− 0.195 |

**5.**    $25 − $13.75 =         5.3 − 2.148 =          394.2 − 181.004 =

**6.**    $14 − $7.95 =          $38 − $27.99 =         365 − 99.559 =

# Adding and Subtracting Decimals
Skill Practice

Find the answer to each decimal problem. Match the letter from the answer to solve the hidden message below. Not all letters are used.

(**!**) 3.7 + 15.09    (**A**) 19.5 − 0.72    (**O**) 9.45 − 0.92    (**E**) 7.1 + 28.55

(**N**) 54 + 126.09    (**R**) 11.5 − 0.863    (**M**) 49.15 + 7.8    (**P**) 38.5 + 9.5 + 0.7

(**Y**) 74 − 68.96    (**I**) 0.92 + 0.946    (**U**) 0.45 − 0.28    (**S**) 51.007 − 3.049

(**L**) 12 − 0.75    (**C**) 1.05 − 0.13    (**D**) 2.3 + 65.81    (**T**) 2.615 + 89.03

| 11.25 | 1.866 | 180.09 | 35.65 | | 0.17 | 48.7 |

| 5.04 | 8.53 | 0.17 | 10.637 |

| 68.11 | 35.65 | 0.92 | 1.866 | 56.95 | 18.78 | 11.25 | 47.958 | 18.79 |

**Math Connection—Grade 6—RBP0180**                    www.summerbridgeactivities.com                    ©RBP Books

# Adding and Subtracting Decimals
Problem Solving—Mind Over Money

Ginny took the money she earned baby-sitting and went to the movies. She spent **$3.90** for her ticket. Then she spent **half** of the remaining money on popcorn. On the way home she bought an ice cream for **$1.49**. When she got home, she had **$0.81** left of her earnings. How much did she earn baby-sitting?

| | | |
|---|---|---|
| $0.81 | → | Start with money left over. |
| + 1.49 | → | Add money spent on ice cream cone. |
| 2.30 | → | Half of remaining money. |
| + 2.30 | → | Add other half of money spent on popcorn. |
| 4.60 | → | Money remaining after buying ticket. |
| + 3.90 | → | Add money spent on ticket. |
| **$8.50** | → | **Money that Ginny earned baby-sitting.** |

1. An owner of a retail clothing store bought a dress for $36.25 and sold it for $59.99. What was her profit? Hint: A *profit* is what you make after you take out your expenses.

2. A pair of running shoes costs $22.29. The store owner wanted to make a profit of $18.50. What should the selling price be?

3. Malcolm spent $48.74 on new speakers and $25.39 on computer games. When he was finished, he only had $0.58 left. How much money did Malcolm have before he went shopping?

4. In the town of Sleepy Oak, the fine for a speeding ticket is $32.65 + s dollars, where s is the miles per hour over the speed limit.

   a. What is the fine for going 38.4 miles per hour in a 25-mile-per-hour school zone? Hint: First find out how many miles over the speed limit 38.4 is.

   **Clue:** Solve a simpler problem.

   b. Mr. Thomas was fined $50.15 for speeding in this school zone. How fast was he driving? Hint: First find the difference between Mr. Thomas's fine and the base fine of $32.65.

5. Hailey received some cash for her birthday. She spent $14.48 on a CD and donated $25 to charity. She put half of what was left into her savings account. She has $17.76 left. How much did she receive on her birthday?

   **Clue:** Work backwards.

www.summerbridgeactivities.com                    **Math Connection—Grade 6—RBP0180**

# Adding and Subtracting Decimals
Problem Solving

1. To make the swim team, Pedro must swim 400 meters in less than 7 minutes. Pedro swam the first 200 meters in 2.86 minutes. He swam the second 200 meters in 3.95 minutes. What is the total amount of time he took to swim 400 meters? Did Pedro make the team?

2. The school record for the 400-meter track relay was 65.5 seconds. This year's Speedsters would like to tie or break the record. It took them 53.96 seconds to run 300 meters. In how much time must they run the last 100 meters to tie the record?

> **FYI:**
> Each person in a 400-meter relay runs 100 meters.

3. The Whiz Kids ran the 400-meter relay in 47.35 seconds. Their time for the first 300 meters was 35.58 seconds. What was their time for the last 100 meters?

Jamie used her pedometer to keep track of how far she walked every week in July. Use the table she made to solve problems 4–6.

| July Walking Distance in Miles | |
|---|---|
| Week 1 | 7.94 |
| Week 2 | 13.7 |
| Week 3 | 9.3 |
| Week 4 | 11.25 |

4. During which two weeks did Jamie's distance total about 19 miles?

5. What is the total distance that Jamie walked in July?

6. Jamie walked 21.7 miles during the month of August. How many miles did she walk during July and August combined?

7. At a track-and-field meet, the winner of the pole-vault event cleared a height of 3.25 meters. This was 0.1 meters more than the height cleared by the second-place pole-vaulter. The second-place height was 0.05 meters more than the third-place height. What height did the third-place pole-vaulter clear?

8. Chung noticed a pattern in his long-jump distances. So far they have been 3.2 meters, 3.325 meters, 3.45 meters, and 3.575 meters. Find Chung's pattern. What is the next distance in his pattern?

> **Clue:**
> Find a pattern.

# Post-Test: Adding and Subtracting Decimals

## Add or subtract.

1.
```
        0.6              6.247            24.2
      + 0.19           + 3.43            1.143
      _____           _____          + 3.004
                                        _____
```

2.
```
       0.48             6.043           14.267
     − 0.07           − 0.011          − 3.102
     _____           _____          _____
```

3.
```
       0.74             6.764           18.7
     + 0.6            + 4.8             8.69
     _____           _____         + 24.048
                                      _____
```

4.
```
      0.321            5                18.2
    − 0.27           − 3.058          − 9.485
    _____           _____          _____
```

## Solve each problem.

5. Huan brought some money to spend on his vacation. On the first day he spent $4.30. On the second day he spent half the money he had left. On the third day, he spent $1.85. He then had $2 left. How much money did Huan start with?

6. The school record in the relay race was 46.2 seconds. This year the record was broken by 0.9 seconds. What was the time this year?

# Pre-Test: Multiplying Decimals

## Find each product.

1.
$$\begin{array}{r} 0.09 \\ \times\ \ 23 \\ \hline \end{array}$$
$$\begin{array}{r} 0.8 \\ \times\ 0.6 \\ \hline \end{array}$$
$$\begin{array}{r} 0.337 \\ \times\ \ \ 0.5 \\ \hline \end{array}$$
$$\begin{array}{r} 1.48 \\ \times\ 0.36 \\ \hline \end{array}$$

2.
$$\begin{array}{r} 0.03 \\ \times\ 0.8 \\ \hline \end{array}$$
$$\begin{array}{r} 0.045 \\ \times\ \ \ 0.2 \\ \hline \end{array}$$
$$\begin{array}{r} 2.98 \\ \times\ 0.05 \\ \hline \end{array}$$
$$\begin{array}{r} 7.34 \\ \times\ 0.003 \\ \hline \end{array}$$

3.
$$\begin{array}{r} 0.6 \\ \times\ 0.37 \\ \hline \end{array}$$
$$\begin{array}{r} 3.43 \\ \times\ \ 0.6 \\ \hline \end{array}$$
$$\begin{array}{r} 7.4 \\ \times\ 5.1 \\ \hline \end{array}$$
$$\begin{array}{r} 0.081 \\ \times\ \ 0.09 \\ \hline \end{array}$$

4.    $10 \times 7.2 =$         $0.481 \times 100 =$         $1,000 \times 0.59 =$

## Solve each problem.

**5.** A tube of toothpaste holds 6.4 ounces. How much toothpaste do 10 tubes hold?

**6.** Keith buys 2.4 pounds of apples at $0.89 per pound. How much do the apples cost?

**Math Connection—Grade 6—RBP0180**          www.summerbridgeactivities.com          ©RBP Books

# Multiplying Decimals
Placing the Decimal Point

To multiply decimals, first multiply the same as you would with whole numbers. Then count the total number of decimal places to the right of the decimal point in each factor. That is the number of decimal places in the product.

---

**Examples:**

| | | |
|---|---|---|
| 4.**69** ← **2** decimal places | 0.**3** ← **1** decimal places | 0.**54** ← **2** decimal places |
| x   3 ← **+0** decimal places | x 8.**72** ← **+2** decimal places | x 0.**38** ← **+2** decimal places |
| 14.**07** ← **2** decimal places | 2.**616** ← **3** decimal places | 0.**2052** ← **4** decimal places |
| ↑ | ↑ | ↑ |
| Place decimal point here. | Place decimal point here. | Place decimal point here. |

---

## Place the decimal point in each answer.

**1.**

| 199.6 | 19.96 | 1.996 | 199.6 | 1.996 |
|---|---|---|---|---|
| x   8 | x   8 | x   8 | x   0.8 | x   0.8 |
| 15968 | 15968 | 15968 | 15968 | 15968 |

**2.**

| 300.4 | 30.04 | 3.004 | 300.4 | 3.004 |
|---|---|---|---|---|
| x   6 | x   6 | x   6 | x   0.6 | x   0.6 |
| 18024 | 18024 | 18024 | 18024 | 18024 |

**3.**

| 250.2 | 25.02 | 2.502 | 250.2 | 2.502 |
|---|---|---|---|---|
| x   5 | x   5 | x   5 | x   0.5 | x   0.5 |
| 12510 | 12510 | 12510 | 12510 | 12510 |

**4.**

| 26.4 | 42.6 | 18.7 | 21.9 | 19.4 |
|---|---|---|---|---|
| x 0.3 | x 0.6 | x 0.7 | x 0.4 | x 3.6 |
| 792 | 2556 | 1309 | 876 | 6984 |

**5.**

| 21.7 | 63.1 | 36.6 | 3.41 | 7.67 |
|---|---|---|---|---|
| x 4.2 | x 2.2 | x 4.7 | x 6.2 | x 1.3 |
| 9114 | 13882 | 17202 | 21142 | 9971 |

**6.**

| 21.43 | 18.72 | 24.062 | 62.003 | 18.417 |
|---|---|---|---|---|
| x   3.04 | x   2.17 | x   1.3 | x   1.4 | x   0.2 |
| 651472 | 406224 | 312806 | 868042 | 36834 |

www.summerbridgeactivities.com

# Multiplying Decimals

Multiply **32 x 0.43**

**Step 1**
Multiply the factors as if the decimal point weren't there.

$$
\begin{array}{r}
32 \\
\times\ 0.43 \\
\hline
96 \\
+\ 1280 \\
\hline
\mathbf{1376}
\end{array}
$$

**Step 2**
Count the number of decimal places.
Then add the decimal point to the product.

$$
\begin{array}{r}
32 \\
\times\ 0.43 \\
\hline
96 \\
+\ 1280 \\
\hline
13.76
\end{array}
$$

32 ← **0** decimal places
x 0.43 ← **2** decimal places

13.**76** ← **2** decimal places in all

**Remember:** Count the decimal places to the right of the decimal.

## Find each product.

**1.**

$$
\begin{array}{r} 0.4 \\ \times\ 6 \\ \hline \end{array}
\qquad
\begin{array}{r} 0.9 \\ \times\ 3 \\ \hline \end{array}
\qquad
\begin{array}{r} 0.12 \\ \times\ 7 \\ \hline \end{array}
\qquad
\begin{array}{r} 4.9 \\ \times\ 8 \\ \hline \end{array}
$$

**2.**

$$
\begin{array}{r} 4.5 \\ \times\ 3 \\ \hline \end{array}
\qquad
\begin{array}{r} 2.81 \\ \times\ 4 \\ \hline \end{array}
\qquad
\begin{array}{r} 1.76 \\ \times\ 5 \\ \hline \end{array}
\qquad
\begin{array}{r} 3.03 \\ \times\ 6 \\ \hline \end{array}
$$

**3.**

$$
\begin{array}{r} 2.8 \\ \times\ 34 \\ \hline \end{array}
\qquad
\begin{array}{r} 6.2 \\ \times\ 13 \\ \hline \end{array}
\qquad
\begin{array}{r} 3.7 \\ \times\ 65 \\ \hline \end{array}
\qquad
\begin{array}{r} 0.17 \\ \times\ 14 \\ \hline \end{array}
$$

**4.**

$$
\begin{array}{r} 0.52 \\ \times\ 26 \\ \hline \end{array}
\qquad
\begin{array}{r} 0.208 \\ \times\ 21 \\ \hline \end{array}
\qquad
\begin{array}{r} 0.836 \\ \times\ 52 \\ \hline \end{array}
\qquad
\begin{array}{r} 0.92 \\ \times\ 27 \\ \hline \end{array}
$$

**5.**

$$
\begin{array}{r} 9.909 \\ \times\ 54 \\ \hline \end{array}
\qquad
\begin{array}{r} 302.6 \\ \times\ 83 \\ \hline \end{array}
\qquad
\begin{array}{r} 3.208 \\ \times\ 91 \\ \hline \end{array}
\qquad
\begin{array}{r} 5.634 \\ \times\ 49 \\ \hline \end{array}
$$

# Multiplying Decimals
Multiplying a Decimal by a Decimal

**Remember:** Multiply as you would with whole numbers. Add up the number of decimal places in both factors. The answer will have the total number of decimal places in the factors.

| Multiply **1.4 x 0.2** | | Multiply **2.53 x 3.1** | |
|---|---|---|---|
| 1.4 ← **1** decimal place | | 2.**53** ← **2** decimal places | |
| x 0.2 ← **1** decimal place | | x 3.1 ← **1** decimal place | |
| 0.**28** ← **2** decimal places | | 253 | |
| | | + 7590 | |
| | | **7.843** ← **3** decimal places in all | |

## Multiply.

**1.**   0.7          0.3          0.54         2.9
       x 0.4        x 0.5        x 0.6        x 5.4


**2.**   8.4          0.7          0.9          0.12
       x 0.6        x 0.12       x 0.2        x 0.22


**3.**   56.1         0.45         0.724        0.46
       x 2.1        x 0.9        x 0.6        x 0.87


**4.**   4.95         0.2          9.12         65.1
       x 0.3        x 7.8        x 4.3        x 0.25


**5.**   3.21         4.7          10.16        24.99
       x 0.8        x 12.5       x 2.21       x 0.52

# Multiplying Decimals
Multiplying Decimals with Zeros in the Product

Multiply **1.05 x 0.03**

| **Step 1** | **Step 2** |
|---|---|
| Multiply as you would with whole numbers. | Count the number of decimal places. Then place the decimal point in your answer. Write zeros to show the extra places. |

**Step 1**
Multiply as you would with whole numbers.

$$\begin{array}{r} 1 \\ 1.05 \\ \times\,0.03 \\ \hline 315 \end{array}$$

**Step 2**
Count the number of decimal places. Then place the decimal point in your answer. Write zeros to show the extra places.

$$\begin{array}{r} 1 \\ 1.05 \\ \times\,0.03 \\ \hline 0.0315 \end{array}$$

1.05 ← **2** decimal places
x 0.03 ← **2** decimal places
0.0315 ← **4** decimal places needed in answer, but only 3 numbers

**Add a zero as placeholder.**

## Multiply.

1.  
$$\begin{array}{r}0.091\\ \times\,0.02\\ \hline\end{array}\qquad \begin{array}{r}0.0072\\ \times\,0.07\\ \hline\end{array}\qquad \begin{array}{r}0.0043\\ \times\,0.9\\ \hline\end{array}\qquad \begin{array}{r}0.025\\ \times\,0.04\\ \hline\end{array}$$

2.  
$$\begin{array}{r}0.33\\ \times\,0.0053\\ \hline\end{array}\qquad \begin{array}{r}0.14\\ \times\,0.0048\\ \hline\end{array}\qquad \begin{array}{r}0.305\\ \times\,0.008\\ \hline\end{array}\qquad \begin{array}{r}0.45\\ \times\,0.007\\ \hline\end{array}$$

3.  
$$\begin{array}{r}0.165\\ \times\,0.08\\ \hline\end{array}\qquad \begin{array}{r}9.7\\ \times\,0.002\\ \hline\end{array}\qquad \begin{array}{r}0.025\\ \times\,0.6\\ \hline\end{array}\qquad \begin{array}{r}0.057\\ \times\,0.43\\ \hline\end{array}$$

4.  
$$\begin{array}{r}0.092\\ \times\,0.086\\ \hline\end{array}\qquad \begin{array}{r}0.125\\ \times\,.023\\ \hline\end{array}\qquad \begin{array}{r}0.0047\\ \times\,0.83\\ \hline\end{array}\qquad \begin{array}{r}0.309\\ \times\,0.09\\ \hline\end{array}$$

5.  
$$\begin{array}{r}0.103\\ \times\,0.005\\ \hline\end{array}\qquad \begin{array}{r}0.017\\ \times\,0.17\\ \hline\end{array}\qquad \begin{array}{r}0.0096\\ \times\,0.37\\ \hline\end{array}\qquad \begin{array}{r}0.031\\ \times\,0.022\\ \hline\end{array}$$

Math Connection—Grade 6—RBP0180          www.summerbridgeactivities.com          © RBP Books

## Multiplying Decimals
Puzzle Practice

# Why are fish so good at math?

To find out, multiply. Then match each letter to its answer in the blanks below. One answer is not used. Remember to write the extra zeros when necessary.

| L  0.033 <br> x  0.2 | Y  0.33 <br> x  0.2 | L  0.47 <br> x 0.2 | A  0.47 <br> x 0.02 |
|---|---|---|---|
| O  0.006 <br> x 0.34 | S  0.06 <br> x 0.34 | I  6 <br> x 0.034 | C  6 <br> x 0.34 |
| W  0.098 <br> x 0.55 | N  0.098 <br> x 0.055 | A  0.082 <br> x 0.063 | O  0.82 <br> x 0.063 |
| S  0.345 <br> x 0.07 | A  0.532 <br> x 0.06 | R  1.75 <br> x .005 | H  0.262 <br> x .004 |

**They  are**  _____  _____  _____  _____  _____  _____
            0.0094    0.094    0.0539    0.005166    0.066    0.0204

_____   _____           _____
0.204    0.00539          0.03192

_____   _____   _____   _____   _____   _____
0.02415   2.04   0.001048   0.05166   0.00204   0.094

# Multiplying Decimals

Mental Math for Multiplying a Decimal by 10, 100, or 1,000

| To multiply by 10, move the decimal point **one** place to the right. | To multiply by 100, move the decimal point **two** places to the right. | To multiply by 1,000, move the decimal point **three** places to the right. |
|---|---|---|
| **0.4** | **0.40** | **0.400** |
| 10 x 0.4 = 4 | 100 x 0.4 = 40 | 1000 x 0.4 = 400 |

## Find each product. Use mental math.

1.  10 x 00.6 =        100 x 0.06 =        1,000 x 0.06 =        10 x 0.6 =

2.  10 x 4.3 =         100 x 4.3 =         1,000 x 4.3 =         0.43 x 100 =

3.  0.653 x 1,000 =    1.09 x 10 =         21.3 x 10 =          10 x 0.007 =

4.  1,000 x 0.046 =    0.46 x 1,000 =      0.46 x 100 =         0.46 x 10 =

5.  1,000 x 3.9 =      0.0045 x 10 =       100 x 0.03 =         12.6 x 1,000 =

6.  1.234 x 100 =      0.11 x 1,000 =      0.11 x 10,000 =      0.11 x 100,000 =

Math Connection—Grade 6—RBP0180                    www.summerbridgeactivities.com            ©RBP Books

# Multiplying Decimals

Multiplication Mania—Practice Your Skills with a Challenge!
Hint: You can guess and check if you get stumped.

## Find the missing digits in the following multiplication problems.

Then place the decimal point in the product.

1.

```
    ☐.88
  x ☐.2
   376
 + 1880
  2256
```

```
    ☐.19
  x 0.3☐
   1038
 + 15570
  16608
```

2.

```
    8.☐6
  x  ☐.3
   2628
 + 35040
  37668
```

```
    ☐5.6
  x   ☐.1
    256
 + 7680
  7936
```

3.

```
    4.☐☐
  x   2.☐
   432
 + 8640
  9072
```

```
    ☐4.9
  x   2.☐
   1043
 + 2980
  4023
```

4.

```
    ☐.5☐
  x ☐.5
   755
 + 6040
  6795
```

```
    ☐.12
  x 0.☐1
   312
 + 18720
  19032
```

# Multiplying Decimals
Problem Solving—Westward Ho

## Solve each problem.

1. A covered wagon on the Oregon trail could travel about 2.5 miles an hour on flat terrain. About how many miles could it travel in 9 hours?

   The covered wagon could travel _____ miles.

2. Pony Express riders of the Old West normally carried about 1,000 letters, each weighing 0.0375 pounds. How many pounds of letters did the Pony Express riders carry?

   The Pony Express could carry _____ pounds of letters.

3. In 1860, gingham cloth sold for $0.25 a yard. Mrs. Olsen bought 16.5 yards to make clothes for her family. How much did she spend on cloth?

   Mrs. Olsen spent $_____ on cloth.

4. In 1863 in Fort Laramie, Wyoming, travelers could buy beef jerky at the trading post for $0.35 per pound. How much would a 16-pound box of jerky cost?

   A 16-pound box of jerky would cost _____.

5. In 1838, the Olsen family traveled through Ohio by canal in 18.5 hours. The Parley Company of travelers took 2.3 times as long to go the same distance over land with their wagons. How long did it take the Parley Company?

   It took the Parley Company _____ hours to go the same distance.

6. In 1865, pioneer travelers could buy wheat for $0.12 a pound at merchant stops along the Oregon trail. The Olsens had a barrel that could hold 19.25 pounds of wheat. How much did it cost to fill the barrel?

   It cost $_____ to fill the barrel with wheat.

7. Each wagon in the Parley Company wagon train was about 3.65 meters long. If 10 wagons traveled end to end, how long would the wagon train be?

   The wagon train would be _____ meters long.

8. If a wagon wheel travels 0.02 km in one revolution, how many km will the wheel have traveled after 1,190 revolutions?

   It would have traveled _____ km.

# Multiplying Decimals
Problem Solving

## Solve each problem.

Mike is in college studying to become a nurse. In many of his laboratory classes, he must measure quantities and record data in his notebooks.

1. Mike performed blood tests using 5 test tubes. Each tube contained 12.73 milliliters (ml) of blood. How much blood did he test total?

   He tested _____ ml total.

2. Mike's lab partner was using a mixture of water and iodine in 8 beakers. Each beaker had 7.012 milliliters of the mixture in it. How much of the mixture did he have altogether?

   He had _____ ml altogether.

3. Mike wrapped a cloth bandage around a patient's arm, turning the bandage 15 times before making it secure. He used 9.12 cm each time he turned the bandage. About how long was the bandage he used?

   The bandage was about _____ cm.

4. In chemistry class, Mike took a package of salt and split the contents evenly into 9 experimental groups. Each group weighed 0.07 kilograms (kg). How much salt was in the original package?

   There was _____ kg of salt in the original package.

5. In his dietary nutrition class, Mike studied nutrition labels on food. A candy bar label read 12.4 grams of fat. If 1 gram of fat contains 9.4 calories, how many calories from fat are in the candy bar?

   There are _____ calories from fat.

6. In biology, Mike wants to view a specimen under a powerful microscope. The specimen is 0.021 cm wide. The microscope will magnify the specimen 100 times larger. How wide will the specimen appear when it is viewed under the microscope?

   The specimen will appear to be _____ cm wide under the microscope.

© RBP Books          www.summerbridgeactivities.com          Math Connection—Grade 6—RBP0180

# Post-Test: Multiplying Decimals

## Find each product.

1.
$$\begin{array}{r} 0.07 \\ \times\ 18 \\ \hline \end{array}$$
$$\begin{array}{r} 0.7 \\ \times\ 0.6 \\ \hline \end{array}$$
$$\begin{array}{r} 0.258 \\ \times\ \ 0.4 \\ \hline \end{array}$$
$$\begin{array}{r} 3.14 \\ \times\ 0.86 \\ \hline \end{array}$$

2.
$$\begin{array}{r} 0.07 \\ \times\ 0.9 \\ \hline \end{array}$$
$$\begin{array}{r} 0.075 \\ \times\ \ 0.4 \\ \hline \end{array}$$
$$\begin{array}{r} 2.87 \\ \times\ 0.05 \\ \hline \end{array}$$
$$\begin{array}{r} 9.26 \\ \times\ 0.003 \\ \hline \end{array}$$

3.
$$\begin{array}{r} 0.9 \\ \times\ 0.27 \\ \hline \end{array}$$
$$\begin{array}{r} 2.54 \\ \times\ \ 0.7 \\ \hline \end{array}$$
$$\begin{array}{r} 8.3 \\ \times\ 9.2 \\ \hline \end{array}$$
$$\begin{array}{r} 0.062 \\ \times\ \ 0.03 \\ \hline \end{array}$$

4.    $10 \times 3.9 =$          $0.463 \times 100 =$          $1,000 \times 0.92 =$

## Solve each problem.

5. A machine part weighs 1.34 ounces. How much do 100 of the same parts weigh?

6. In the turtle trot race, a turtle travels at a rate of 0.09 miles per hour. How far will the turtle travel in 0.40 hours?

# Pre-Test: Dividing Decimals

## Divide.

1. $8 \overline{)7.2}$      $18 \overline{)7.56}$      $6 \overline{)1.38}$      $35 \overline{)74.9}$

2. $4 \overline{)32.12}$      $14 \overline{)70.98}$      $36 \overline{)0.324}$      $58 \overline{)0.3654}$

3. $0.6 \overline{)0.048}$      $0.56 \overline{)1.288}$      $0.8 \overline{)184}$      $0.25 \overline{)9}$

4.      $4.18 \div 10 =$          $60.5 \div 100 =$          $93.6 \div 1,000 =$

## Write each fraction as a decimal by dividing.

5.    $\dfrac{3}{25}$          $\dfrac{7}{8}$          $\dfrac{18}{125}$          $\dfrac{125}{200}$

## Solve each problem.

6. An 11-ounce bottle of shampoo costs $2.97. What is the cost per ounce?

7. A 10-story building is 127.5 feet high. How tall is each story if they are all the same height?

# Dividing Decimals by Whole Numbers

Divide **3.25 ÷ 5**

---

**Step 1**
Place the decimal point in the quotient directly above the decimal point in the dividend.

$$5 \overline{)3.25}$$

**Remember:**
The **dividend** is 3.25 because it is the number that is to be <u>divided</u>.

**Step 2**
Then, divide as you would whole numbers.

$$\begin{array}{r} 0.65 \\ 5\overline{)3.25} \\ -30 \phantom{0} \\ \hline 25 \\ -25 \\ \hline 0 \end{array}$$

**Step 3**
Check by multiplying.

$$5\overline{)3.25}^{\,0.65}$$

$$\begin{array}{r} 0.65 \\ \times \quad 5 \\ \hline 3.25 \end{array}$$

---

## Divide. Check your work.

1.  $8\overline{)2.4}$        $8\overline{)0.24}$        $3\overline{)0.69}$        $3\overline{)0.069}$

2.  $2\overline{)45.4}$        $2\overline{)4.54}$        $7\overline{)\$34.37}$        $5\overline{)0.105}$

3.  $6\overline{)120.6}$        $6\overline{)12.06}$        $4\overline{)2.44}$        $6\overline{)\$2.76}$

4.  $6\overline{)5.88}$        $4\overline{)7.36}$        $8\overline{)7.592}$        $8\overline{)\$10.40}$

5.  $6\overline{)0.6732}$        $8\overline{)68.328}$        $5\overline{)\$543.20}$        $7\overline{)0.266}$

Math Connection—Grade 6—RBP0180          www.summerbridgeactivities.com          ©RBP Books

# Dividing Decimals: Zeros in the Dividend

Divide **2.5 ÷ 4**

---

| **Step 1** Divide the tenths. | **Step 2** Write a 0 in the hundredths place. | **Step 3** Write another **0** in the thousandths place. Bring down and divide. |
|---|---|---|
| $$\begin{array}{r} 0.6 \\ 4\overline{)2.5} \\ -2\,4 \\ \hline 1 \end{array}$$ | $$\begin{array}{r} 0.62 \\ 4\overline{)2.50} \\ -2\,4 \\ \hline 10 \\ -8 \\ \hline 2 \end{array}$$ ← Write a zero here. ← Write a zero here. Divide by 4. | $$\begin{array}{r} 0.625 \\ 4\overline{)2.500} \\ -2\,4 \\ \hline 10 \\ -8 \\ \hline 20 \\ -20 \\ \hline 0 \end{array}$$ |

## Divide. Check your work.

---

1.  $5\overline{)2.7}$     $4\overline{)4.6}$     $6\overline{)5.7}$     $4\overline{)7.3}$     $8\overline{)2.5}$

2.  $4\overline{)0.31}$    $5\overline{)8.1}$     $4\overline{)6.3}$     $5\overline{)0.73}$    $4\overline{)4.2}$

3.  $5\overline{)4.19}$    $5\overline{)3.74}$    $4\overline{)53.4}$    $2\overline{)0.113}$   $5\overline{)75.02}$

4.  $18\overline{)9.63}$   $40\overline{)53.6}$   $16\overline{)5.2}$    $32\overline{)6.8}$    $56\overline{)9.8}$

# Dividing Decimals: Zeros in the Quotient

Divide **0.192 ÷ 32**

$$32\overline{)0.192}$$  ←  First, put the decimal point in the **quotient** directly above the decimal point in the dividend.

Then divide.

$$32\overline{)0.192}^{\,0.0}$$

There are no 32's in 1.

$$32\overline{)0.192}^{\,0.00}$$

There are no 32's in 19.

$$
\begin{array}{r}
0.006 \\
32\overline{)0.192} \\
-192 \\
\hline
0
\end{array}
$$

There are 6 32's in 192.

## Divide. Check your work.

1. $4\overline{)2.8}$    $7\overline{)0.56}$    $2\overline{)0.018}$    $3\overline{)0.21}$    $6\overline{)0.096}$

2. $8\overline{)0.52}$    $8\overline{)0.19}$    $5\overline{)0.451}$    $6\overline{)0.1065}$    $4\overline{)0.38}$

3. $24\overline{)0.15}$    $65\overline{)1.95}$    $10\overline{)62.4}$    $29\overline{)0.174}$    $71\overline{)0.923}$

4. $31\overline{)0.6417}$    $12\overline{)0.42}$    $27\overline{)94.5}$    $59\overline{)1.947}$    $73\overline{)0.6205}$

**Math Connection—Grade 6—RBP0180**                www.summerbridgeactivities.com                ©RBP Books

# Dividing by a Decimal

To divide by a decimal number, you must move the decimal to make the **divisor** a whole number. To make the divisor a whole number, multiply both the divisor and dividend by 10, 100, or 1,000.

**Example:** $0.08\overline{)6.081}$ = $8\overline{)608.1}$

Divide **5.44 ÷ 1.6**

**Step 1**
Move the decimal point one place to the right to make the divisor a whole number.

$1.6\overline{)5.44}$  ◄— Multiply by 10.

**Step 2**
Place the decimal point in the quotient. Divide as you would with whole numbers.

$$
\begin{array}{r}
3.4 \\
16\overline{)54.4} \\
-48\phantom{.4} \\
\hline
64 \\
-64 \\
\hline
0
\end{array}
$$

**Remember:**
The **divisor** is 1.6 because it is the number you are dividing into the dividend.

## Divide. Check your work.

1. $0.6\overline{)5.4}$    $0.9\overline{)0.18}$    $1.4\overline{)13.86}$    $0.86\overline{)0.688}$

2. $1.7\overline{)10.54}$    $2.4\overline{)16.8}$    $0.07\overline{)0.035}$    $0.92\overline{)0.736}$

3. $0.005\overline{)0.015}$    $3.2\overline{)13.76}$    $0.63\overline{)0.441}$    $0.086\overline{)0.0258}$

4. $0.4\overline{)0.856}$    $2.8\overline{)2.716}$    $0.37\overline{)0.3108}$    $0.65\overline{)0.1105}$

# Dividing by a Decimal

Sometimes you may need to add zeros to the dividend.

**Examples:**

$0.003\overline{)12}$

$0.003\overline{)12.000}$

$$
\begin{array}{r}
4,000 \\
3\overline{)12000} \\
-12\phantom{000} \\
\hline
0000 \\
0000 \\
\hline
0 \\
\end{array}
$$

$0.65\overline{)14.3}$

$0.65\overline{)14.30}$

$$
\begin{array}{r}
22 \\
65\overline{)1430} \\
-130\phantom{0} \\
\hline
130 \\
-130 \\
\hline
0 \\
\end{array}
$$

## Divide. Check your work.

1.  $0.5\overline{)255}$    $0.016\overline{)0.8}$    $0.45\overline{)9}$    $0.045\overline{)90}$

2.  $0.4\overline{)85}$    $0.6\overline{)261}$    $0.8\overline{)476}$    $0.24\overline{)11.7}$

3.  $0.48\overline{)16.8}$    $3.5\overline{)119}$    $0.72\overline{)3.6}$    $0.25\overline{)6}$

4.  $.02\overline{)9.5}$    $0.5\overline{)23.6}$    $0.51\overline{)163.2}$    $0.46\overline{)82.8}$

5.  $0.14\overline{)11.9}$    $0.02\overline{)0.16}$    $0.3\overline{)28.2}$    $0.002\overline{)0.06}$

**Math Connection—Grade 6—RBP0180**    www.summerbridgeactivities.com    ©RBP Books

# Dividing Decimals
Mental Math for Dividing by 10, 100, or 1,000

| To divide by 10, move the decimal point in the dividend **one** place to the left. The result is your quotient. | To divide by 100, move the decimal point in the dividend **two** places to the left. The result is your quotient. | To divide by 1,000, move the decimal point in the dividend **three** places to the left. The result is your quotient. |
|---|---|---|
| $315 \div 10 = $ **31.5** | $315 \div 100 = $ **3.15** | $315 \div 1000 = $ **.315** |
| 315. | 315. | 315. |

## Find each quotient. Use mental math.

1.    $40.5 \div 100 = $      $2.5 \div 1,000 = $      $70.3 \div 100 = $      $0.03 \div 10 = $

2.    $983 \div 100 = $      $90.9 \div 100 = $      $4,518 \div 100 = $      $38,693 \div 100 = $

3.    $88.56 \div 10 = $      $0.009 \div 100 = $      $0.75 \div 1,000 = $      $0.057 \div 100 = $

4.    $7.03 \div 1,000 = $      $74.41 \div 10 = $      $2.301 \div 100 = $      $320.16 \div 1,000 = $

5.    $9.125 \div 10 = $      $6,392 \div 100 = $      $7,452 \div 1,000 = $      $25,125 \div 100 = $

6.    $478.5 \div 1,000 = $      $0.235 \div 10 = $      $45.42 \div 100 = $      $3.667 \div 10 = $

## Expressing Fractions as Decimals: Revisited

Another way to write a fraction as a decimal is to divide the numerator by the denominator.

**Example:** $\frac{5}{8} = 5 \div 8$

```
        0.625
   8 ) 5.000   ← Remember that you may need to add zeros to carry out the division.
     − 48
       20
      − 16
       40
      − 40
        0    So, 5/8 = .625
```

## Write each fraction as a decimal by dividing the numerator by the denominator.

| | | | | | |
|---|---|---|---|---|---|
| **1.** | $\frac{4}{5}$ | $\frac{3}{8}$ | $\frac{3}{5}$ | $\frac{9}{15}$ | $\frac{19}{25}$ |
| **2.** | $\frac{17}{20}$ | $\frac{1}{25}$ | $\frac{9}{40}$ | $\frac{18}{25}$ | $\frac{3}{16}$ |
| **3.** | $\frac{111}{200}$ | $\frac{5}{16}$ | $\frac{45}{200}$ | $\frac{8}{25}$ | $\frac{19}{40}$ |
| **4.** | $\frac{9}{12}$ | $\frac{11}{16}$ | $\frac{4}{8}$ | $\frac{87}{200}$ | $\frac{3}{25}$ |
| **5.** | $\frac{9}{20}$ | $\frac{39}{40}$ | $\frac{12}{32}$ | $\frac{29}{500}$ | $\frac{7}{125}$ |

# Dividing Decimals
Problem Solving—Unit Costs at the Grocery Store

When finding a unit cost, divide the total cost by the number of units:

**$Total Cost ÷ Number of Units = $Unit Cost**

or

$$\text{Number of Units } \overline{)\, \$\text{Total Cost}}^{\$\text{Unit Cost}}$$

**Example:**

Maria bought a **15**-ounce bag of tortilla chips for **$2.25**. What is the cost per ounce?

$$
\begin{array}{r}
0.15 \\
15 \overline{)\, 2.25} \\
-15 \\
\hline
75 \\
-75 \\
\hline
0
\end{array}
$$

Number of Units ⟶ 15 ) 2.25 ⟵ Total Cost

0.15 ⟵ Unit Cost (per ounce)

So, the bag of tortilla chips cost $0.15 per ounce.

## Solve each problem.

1. At Orchard Street Market, 4.5 pounds of pears cost $2.97. What is the cost per pound?

2. Mrs. Parks bought 30 ice cream bars for her daughter's class party. She paid $12.60. How much did each ice cream bar cost?

3. Sandy bought a 32.5-ounce package of mixed nuts for $7.15. What is the cost per ounce?

4. A $2.56 can of lemonade mix will make 64 cups of lemonade. What is the cost per cup?

5. Whole watermelons are sold for $3.99 each. Sonia bought a watermelon that weighed 21 pounds. What price per pound did she pay?

6. A package of 100 napkins costs $2.00. What is the cost per napkin?

# Dividing Decimals
Problem Solving—It's Music to Our Ears!

Did you know that sound energy can be measured in watts? The table shows the energy output of some musical instruments.

| Instrument | Energy Output |
|---|---|
| Piano | .44 watt |
| Trombone | 6.4 watts |
| Snare Drum | 12.3 watts |
| Human Voice | 0.000024 watt |

How many snare drums would it take to produce 73.8 watts of energy?

**Think: 73.8 ÷ 12.3**

$$123 \overline{)738}$$ quotient $6$, $-738$, $0$

So **6** snare drums would produce 73.8 watts of energy.

## Use the table to solve the problems.

1. How many trombones would it take to produce **1,280** watts of energy?

2. A piano can produce **8** times as much sound energy as a flute. How much energy does a flute produce?

3. About how many pianos playing together will produce the same sound energy as one snare drum?

   **Clue:**
   Interpret the remainder. You can't have part of a piano playing. Round to whole numbers.

4. A snare drum, a piano, and a trombone are all playing at once.
   a. What is the combined energy output of the instruments?

   b. What is the average energy output of the instruments?

5. How many pianos would produce **4.84** watts of energy?

6. A trombone can produce **80** times as much sound energy as a piccolo. What is the energy output of a piccolo?

   **Clue:**
   To multiply a number by 1,000,000, move the decimal 6 places to the right.

7. What is the energy output of **1 million** voices?

# Post-Test: Dividing Decimals

## Divide.

1. $9\overline{)5.4}$        $12\overline{)4.44}$        $7\overline{)0.84}$        $52\overline{)71.24}$

2. $8\overline{)40.72}$        $13\overline{)26.39}$        $48\overline{)0.144}$        $43\overline{)0.1591}$

3. $0.7\overline{)0.028}$        $0.43\overline{)0.645}$        $0.4\overline{)72}$        $0.16\overline{)4}$

4. $4.18 \div 10 =$        $60.5 \div 100 =$        $93.6 \div 1{,}000 =$

## Write each fraction as a decimal by dividing.

5. $\dfrac{9}{20}$        $\dfrac{3}{16}$        $\dfrac{50}{125}$        $\dfrac{34}{250}$

## Solve each problem.

6. Jason spent $12.25 for a pack of trading cards. If the pack contains 25 cards, what is the cost per card?

7. A marble factory uses 5,864.7 grams of glass to make 1,000 marbles of the same size. How much does each marble weigh?

# Geometry: Perimeter and Area

The distance around a figure is called its **perimeter**. The perimeter is measured in units of length. The **area** of a figure is the number of square units the figure contains.

Find the perimeter and area of a rectangle with a length of **5 cm** and a width of **3 cm**.

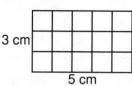

3 cm

5 cm

To find the perimeter:

**Add the sides of the figure.**

**5** cm + **3** cm + **5** cm + **3** cm = **16** cm

or

**Use the formula**    $P = 2l + 2w$

| $l$ = length |
| $w$ = width |
| $P$ = perimeter |

    = $(2 \times 5) + (2 \times 3)$
    = $10 + 6$
    = **16** cm

To find the area:

**Use the formula**    $A = l \times w$

| $l$ = length |
| $w$ = width |
| $P$ = perimeter |

    = 5 cm x 3 cm
    = **15** cm

## Find the perimeter and area of each rectangle with the given length and width.

1.
$l$ = 9 in.
$w$ = 10 in.

P = ___ in.

A = ___ in.

$l$ = 3.5 ft.
$w$ = 2 ft.

P = ___ ft.

A = ___ ft.

$l$ = 5 m
$w$ = 4.5 m

P = ___ m

A = ___ m

2.
$l$ = 10.25 in.
$w$ = 4 in.

P = ___ in.

A = ___ in.

$l$ = 30 yd.
$w$ = 15 yd.

P = ___ yd.

A = ___ yd.

$l$ = 7.3 cm
$w$ = 3.7 cm

P = ___ cm

A = ___ cm

## Find the perimeter and area of each figure.

3.

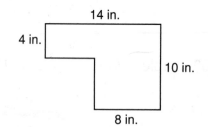

14 in.
4 in.
10 in.
8 in.

P = ___ in.

A = ___ in.$^2$

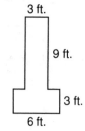

3 ft.
9 ft.
3 ft.
6 ft.

P = ___ ft.

A = ___ ft.$^2$

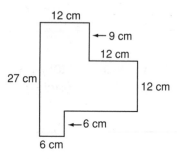

12 cm
9 cm
12 cm
27 cm
12 cm
6 cm
6 cm

P = ___ cm

A = ___ cm$^2$

# Geometry: Area of Triangles and Parallelograms

Find the area of the triangle.

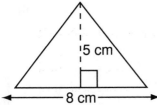

The area (**A**) of the triangle is equal to $\frac{1}{2}$ the base (**b**) times the height (**h**).

$$A = \frac{1}{2} \times b \times h$$

$$A = \frac{1}{2} \times 8 \times 5 = 20$$

The area of the triangle is **20 cm²**

Find the area of the parallelogram.

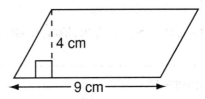

The area (**A**) of the parallelogram is equal to the base (**b**) times the height (**h**).

$$A = b \times h$$

$$A = 9 \times 4 = 36$$

The area of the parallelogram is **36 m²**

## Find the area of each figure.

**1.**

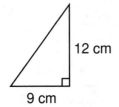

A = _____ cm²

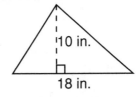

10 in.

20 in.

A = _____ in.²

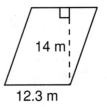

A = _____ ft.²

**2.**

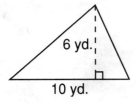

A = _____ yd.²

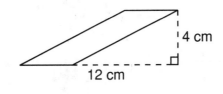

A = _____ cm²

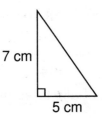

A = _____ cm²

**3.**

A = _____ ft.²

A = _____ in.²

A = _____ m²

**4.** A parallelogram with a base of 3 cm and a height of 1.5 cm.

**5.** A triangle with a base of 12 ft and a height of 4 ft.

www.summerbridgeactivities.com **Math Connection—Grade 6—RBP0180**

# Ratios and Proportions: Writing Ratios

A **ratio** is a comparison of two numbers. One way to write a ratio is by using a fraction.

Roberto's football team **won 7** games and **lost 3** games. The ratio of games won to games lost is read "**7 to 3**."

What is the ratio of games lost to games won?

Compare:  $\dfrac{\text{games lost}}{\text{games won}} \longrightarrow \dfrac{3}{7}$  The ratio is read "**3 to 7**."

**Remember:**
The order in which you compare two numbers of a ratio is important.

## Write the ratio as a fraction as shown.

1. 5 cheetahs to 7 tigers        $\dfrac{5}{7}$        20 tulips to 13 roses        _____

2. 12 trumpets to 5 violins        _____        4 taxis to 9 buses        _____

3. Jill's 23¢ to Bob's 45¢        _____        10 chairs to 3 tables        _____

4. 1 meter to 4 meters        _____        3 min. to 25 min.        _____

## Use the picture. Write a ratio as a fraction for the balls

5. soccer balls to footballs        _____

6. baseballs to soccer balls        _____

7. footballs to soccer balls        _____

8. baseballs to all balls        _____

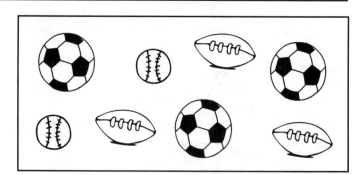

## Use the table to find each ratio.

9. Seattle games won to games lost        _____

10. Kansas City games won to games played        _____

11. Oakland games lost to games played        _____

12. Chicago games lost to games won        _____

13. Texas games won to games lost        _____

| Team | Win | Loss |
|------|-----|------|
| Seattle | 49 | 54 |
| Kansas City | 57 | 47 |
| Oakland | 62 | 42 |
| Chicago | 44 | 60 |
| Texas | 56 | 47 |

# Ratios and Proportions: Equal Ratios

Camille reads **2 books** every **3 weeks**. At that rate, how many books will she read in 12 weeks?

Compare:   $\dfrac{\text{number of books}}{\text{number of weeks}}$ $\longrightarrow$ $\dfrac{2}{3} = \dfrac{n}{12}$ $\longleftarrow$ $\dfrac{\text{books}}{\text{weeks}}$

$\dfrac{2}{3} = \dfrac{2 \times 4}{3 \times 4} = \dfrac{8}{12}$   So, Camille will read **8 books** in 12 weeks.

## Find the missing term.

1.   $\dfrac{5}{6} = \dfrac{n}{36}$ $\qquad$ $\dfrac{3}{8} = \dfrac{n}{24}$ $\qquad$ $\dfrac{5}{7} = \dfrac{n}{42}$ $\qquad$ $\dfrac{8}{9} = \dfrac{n}{63}$

$\quad$ $n =$ _____ $\qquad\qquad$ $n =$ _____ $\qquad\qquad$ $n =$ _____ $\qquad\qquad$ $n =$ _____

## Use equal ratios to find the value of $n$.

2. 9 bars of soap for \$3 = $n$ bars of soap for \$9 $\qquad\qquad$ $n =$ _____

3. 5 points per 2 games = $n$ points per 16 games $\qquad\qquad$ $n =$ _____

4. 10 tickets per child = $n$ tickets per 5 children $\qquad\qquad$ $n =$ _____

5. 52 kilometers per hour = $n$ kilometers per 3 hours $\qquad\qquad$ $n =$ _____

6. 20 people in 4 cars = $n$ people in 8 cars $\qquad\qquad$ $n =$ _____

7. 40 hours in one week = $n$ hours in 10 weeks $\qquad\qquad$ $n =$ _____

8. 4 pounds for 16 people = $n$ pounds for 48 people $\qquad\qquad$ $n =$ _____

9. 60 miles per hour = $n$ miles per 4 hours $\qquad\qquad$ $n =$ _____

10. 25 miles per gallon of gas = $n$ miles per 10 gallons $\qquad\qquad$ $n =$ _____

$\qquad$ www.summerbridgeactivities.com $\qquad$ Math Connection—Grade 6—RBP0180

# Ratios and Proportions: Solving Proportions

An equation showing the equality of two ratios, such as $\frac{3}{7} = \frac{9}{21}$, is called a **proportion**.

The cross products in a proportion are always equal.

    $3 \times 21 = 7 \times 9$

**Here's the official rule:**
In a proportion,

if $\dfrac{a}{b} = \dfrac{c}{d}$

then $a \times d = b \times c$

Find the missing term in the proportion $\frac{2}{5} = \frac{n}{25}$

| **Step 1** | **Step 2** | **Step 3** |
|---|---|---|
| Identify the terms to be multiplied. These are cross products. <br>  | Set up the cross products equal to each other. <br><br> $5 \times n = 2 \times 25$ | Solve. <br><br> $5 \times n = 2 \times 25$ <br> $5 \times n = 50$ <br> $n = 50 \div 5$ <br> $n = \mathbf{10}$ |

## Use cross products to find each proportion.

1.    $\dfrac{5}{2} = \dfrac{10}{m}$       $\dfrac{3}{a} = \dfrac{9}{3}$       $\dfrac{12}{d} = \dfrac{3}{1}$       $\dfrac{7}{n} = \dfrac{2}{4}$

2.    $\dfrac{p}{15} = \dfrac{6}{5}$       $\dfrac{3}{21} = \dfrac{j}{14}$       $\dfrac{120}{30} = \dfrac{s}{5}$       $\dfrac{y}{18} = \dfrac{3}{6}$

3.    $\dfrac{100}{20} = \dfrac{5}{r}$       $\dfrac{24}{k} = \dfrac{8}{12}$       $\dfrac{g}{15} = \dfrac{8}{5}$       $\dfrac{5}{5} = \dfrac{7}{t}$

4.    $\dfrac{12}{5} = \dfrac{24}{b}$       $\dfrac{27}{18} = \dfrac{6}{m}$       $\dfrac{30}{25} = \dfrac{r}{10}$       $\dfrac{n}{21} = \dfrac{2}{14}$

5.    $\dfrac{7}{8} = \dfrac{21}{s}$       $\dfrac{12}{5} = \dfrac{36}{f}$       $\dfrac{100}{v} = \dfrac{10}{12}$       $\dfrac{2}{8} = \dfrac{s}{16}$

*Math Connection—Grade 6—RBP0180*        www.summerbridgeactivities.com        ©RBP Books

# Percents: Percents as Fractions

The number 100 is used in ratios called **percents**.
*Per cent* means *per 100*

The grid contains 100 squares
75 out of 100 squares are shaded.
As a ratio, the shaded part is $\frac{75}{100}$.
As a percent, the shaded part is **75%**.

As a fraction in lowest terms, the shaded part is $\frac{3}{4}$.

$\frac{3}{4} = \frac{n}{100}$

$n = 75$

$\frac{3}{4} = \frac{75}{100} = 75\%$

Think of *cent* words.
*Centennial* is a 100-year celebration.
*Century* is a 100-year period.
One *cent* is $\frac{1}{100}$ of a dollar.
A *centurion* is a person who is 100 years old.

## Write each ratio as a percent.

1. $\frac{79}{100}$      $\frac{5}{100}$      $\frac{27}{100}$      $\frac{50}{100}$

2. $\frac{9}{100}$      $\frac{80}{100}$      $\frac{4}{100}$      $\frac{37}{100}$

3. $\frac{86}{100}$      $\frac{150}{100}$      $\frac{99}{100}$      $\frac{200}{100}$

## Write each percent as a fraction in lowest terms as shown.

4.

| Percent | 25% | 3% | 50% | 33% | 65% | 56% | 30% | 5% | 98% | 7% |
|---|---|---|---|---|---|---|---|---|---|---|
| Equivalent Ratio | $\frac{25}{100}$ | $\frac{3}{100}$ | | | | | | | | |
| Fraction in Lowest Terms | $\frac{1}{4}$ | $\frac{3}{100}$ | | | | | | | | |

## Write each fraction as an equivalent ratio with 100 in the denominator and as a percent.

5.

| Fraction | $\frac{3}{20}$ | $\frac{1}{10}$ | $\frac{3}{5}$ | $\frac{9}{10}$ | $\frac{9}{12}$ | $\frac{4}{40}$ | $\frac{6}{10}$ | $\frac{24}{48}$ | $\frac{1}{50}$ | $\frac{13}{20}$ |
|---|---|---|---|---|---|---|---|---|---|---|
| Equivalent Ratio with 100 as Denominator | $\frac{15}{100}$ | | | | | | | | | |
| Fraction in Lowest Terms | 15% | | | | | | | | | |

# Percents: Percents as Decimals

To change a <u>decimal to a percent,</u> multiply by 100 and write a % sign.

0.36 x 100 = 36%     0.04 x 100 = 4%     0.152 x 100 = 15.2%

> **Remember:**
> To multiply by 100, move the decimal point 2 places to the right.

To change a <u>percent to a decimal</u>, delete the % sign and divide the number by 100.

42% = 0.42          9% = 0.09          23.5% = 0.235

> **Remember:**
> To divide by 100, move the decimal point 2 places to the left.

## Write each decimal as a percent.

| | | | | |
|---|---|---|---|---|
| **1.** | 0.02 = | 0.06 = | 0.01 = | 0.08 = |
| **2.** | 0.10 = | 0.20 = | 0.12 = | 0.24 = |
| **3.** | 0.37 = | 0.69 = | 0.40 = | 0.21 = |
| **4.** | 0.75 = | 0.70 = | 0.25 = | 0.50 = |
| **5.** | 0.999 = | 0.499 = | 1.75 = | 2.25 = |

## Write each percent as a decimal.

| | | | | |
|---|---|---|---|---|
| **6.** | 24% = | 65% = | 88% = | 3% = |
| **7.** | 17% = | 9% = | 10% = | 86% = |
| **8.** | 75% = | 20% = | 4% = | 50% = |
| **9.** | 30% = | 90% = | 5% = | 12% = |
| **10.** | 66.7% = | 33.3% = | 145% = | 210% = |

Math Connection—Grade 6—RBP0180          www.summerbridgeactivities.com          © RBP Books

# Relating Fractions, Decimals, and Percents

## Complete the table with equivalent fractions, decimals, and percents.

Then match each letter to its answer on the blanks below. Not all letters are used.

|    | Fraction | Decimal | Percent |
|----|----------|---------|---------|
| 1. | $\frac{1}{50}$ | .02 = S | = Y |
| 2. | = N | = E | 3% |
| 3. | = N | 0.12 | = E |
| 4. | $\frac{3}{8}$ | = E | = E |
| 5. | = C | 0.35 | = U |
| 6. | = R | 0.45 | = N |
| 7. | = P | = T | 50% |
| 8. | $\frac{18}{25}$ | = T | = N |
| 9. | = I | = A | 90% |
| 10.| = N | 1.0 | 100% |

This means "Almost Perfect."

___  ___  ___  ___  ___  ___    ‾   ___  ___  ___  ___
 1   $\frac{9}{10}$   $\frac{3}{25}$   37.5%   .50   2%       45%   $\frac{9}{10}$   $\frac{3}{100}$   .375

___  ___  ___  ___  ___  ___  ___
$\frac{1}{2}$   12%   $\frac{9}{20}$   $\frac{7}{20}$   0.03   72%   0.72

## Solve the problem.

11. At Wasatch Middle School, $\frac{1}{3}$ of the students are in sixth grade, 35% are in seventh grade, and the rest are in eighth grade.

    a. Which grade has the greatest number of students?

    b. Which grade has the fewest number of students?

www.summerbridgeactivities.com   **Math Connection—Grade 6—RBP0180**

# Percents: Finding the Percent of a Number

Here are two methods you can use to find the percent of a number.

Find **20%** of **130**
Multiply by an equivalent fraction.
$$20\% \text{ of } 130 = 20\% \times 130$$
$$= \frac{20}{100} \times 130$$
$$= \frac{1}{5} \times 130$$
$$= \mathbf{26}$$

Find **4%** of **25**
Multiply by an equivalent decimal.
$$4\% \text{ of } 25 = 4\% \times 25$$
$$= 0.04 \times 25$$

$$
\begin{array}{r}
0.04 \\
\times\ 25 \\
\hline
\end{array}
$$
$$= \mathbf{1.00} \text{ or } \mathbf{1}$$

## Solve using either method.

| | | | |
|---|---|---|---|
| **1.** 3% of 10 = | 4% of 30 = | 16% of 80 = | 15% of 60 = |
| **2.** 18% of 36 = | 6% of 80 = | 9% of 90 = | 11% of 44 = |
| **3.** 8% of 68 = | 9% of 75 = | 62% of 62 = | 44% of 76 = |
| **4.** 4% of 400 = | 3% of 200 = | 37% of 51 = | 28% of 43 = |
| **5.** 1% of 246 = | 5% of 286 = | 60% of 300 = | 40% of 125 = |
| **6.** 120% of 30 = | 150% of 40 = | 125% of 400 = | 108% of 250 = |

# Percents: Finding Discounts and Sale Prices

A **discount** is an amount of decrease from a regular price.
A discounted price is often called a **sale price**.

Find the discount and the sale price for the camera.

| Discount = regular price x discount rate |
|---|
| = $250 x 40% |
| = $250 x 0.4 |
| = **$100** |

| Sale Price = regular price – discount |
|---|
| = $250 - $100 |
| = $150 |

## Complete the table.

| | Regular Price | Discount Rate | Discount | Sale Price |
|---|---|---|---|---|
| 1. | $24 | 40% | $24 x 0.40 = **$9.60** | $24 – $9.60 = **$14.40** |
| 2. | $25 | 30% | $25 x 0.30 = $_____ | $25 – $_____ = $_____ |
| 3. | $80 | 15% | | |
| 4. | $220 | 60% | | |
| 5. | $90 | 55% | | |
| 6. | $120 | 45% | | |
| 7. | $1,250 | 25% | | |
| 8. | $198 | 50% | | |
| 9. | $65 | 15% | | |
| 10. | $4 | 40% | | |
| 11. | $80 | 10% | | |
| 12. | $20 | 35% | | |
| 13. | $6 | 20% | | |
| 14. | $99 | 33% | | |

www.summerbridgeactivities.com
Math Connection—Grade 6—RBP0180

# Using What We Know: Real-Life Problem Solving
Caring for Our Environment

Here are some garbage facts:
- In the United States, 6 out of every 10 aluminum cans are recycled. Each can has a mass or weight of about 1.5 grams.
- Each American throws away about 12.2 pounds of plastic packaging each year.
- Every year, each American throws out about 1,200 pounds of organic garbage like potato peels, watermelon rinds, grass clippings, etc. This type of garbage decomposes and can be used to fertilize the soil.
- Each American on average produces about 1,600 pounds of garbage each year.

## Solve each problem. Use the above information as needed.

1. What percent of aluminum cans are recycled in the United States?

2. For every 100 cans that are recycled, how many grams of aluminum would there be?

3. A plastic milk jug weighs approximately 0.05 pound. If each American throws away 12.2 pounds of plastic each year in the form of milk jugs, how many milk jugs is this?

4. What fraction of each American's yearly garbage is organic waste?

    a. Write this value as a fraction in lowest terms. _____

    b. What decimal is this equivalent to? _____

    c. What percent is this equivalent to? _____

5. Some states pay $0.05 per aluminum can that is recycled. If your family of four drank 24 cans of soda each week (that's one six-pack per person, per week), how much money could you earn in one year by recycling your family's aluminum cans? Hint: There are 52 weeks in one year.

6. Water is another resource that we need to use wisely and not waste. A bath uses about 20 gallons of water. A short shower uses about 15 gallons of water.

    a. What is the ratio of water used in baths to showers? Write this ratio as a fraction in lowest terms. _____

    b. Fill in the blanks with the correct numbers to complete the sentence.

    **For every _____ baths you take, you can take _____ showers and use the same amount of water.**

# Professional Sports

## Solve each problem.

The NBA keeps statistics on points scored per game.
Here is a list of the top 5 scorers in NBA history.

| Player | Average Points per Game |
|--------|------------------------|
| Michael Jordan | 31.1 |
| Wilt Chamberlain | 30.1 |
| Shaquille O' Neal | 27.4 |
| Elgin Baylor | 27.4 |
| Jerry West | 27.0 |

1. What is the **range** of these scores?

 This means, "What is the difference between the highest and lowest average scores?"

2. Based on their averages, about how many points could these five players score in a game?

3. A professional basketball court is a rectangle that is 31.3 yards long and 16.6 yards wide. What is the perimeter of the court? What is the area of the entire basketball court?

   Perimeter = _____ yards        Area = _____ square yards

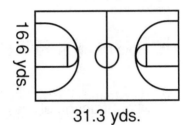

16.6 yds.

31.3 yds.

4. A football field is 100 yards long and 60 yards wide. Use mental math to find the perimeter and area of a football field.

   Perimeter = _____ yards        Area = _____ square yards

5. What is the difference in area between the football field and the basketball court?

6. The National Hockey League awards the Stanley Cup to the league's top team each year. The table shows the teams with the most Stanley Cup wins. Find the mean, median, and mode of this data.

   Mean _____  Median _____  Mode _____

| Team | Number of Stanley Cups Won |
|------|---------------------------|
| Montreal Canadians | 24 |
| Toronto Maple Leafs | 11 |
| Detroit Red Wings | 10 |
| Boston Bruins | 5 |
| Edmonton Oilers | 5 |

7. The Indianapolis 500 is held on a $2\frac{1}{2}$ mile oval track. To win the Indy 500, the driver must be the first to complete 500 miles around the track in his car. How many times do the cars need to circle the track to complete 500 miles?

# The Human Body

Here are some facts about the human body:
- The human body is made of natural elements. Its chemical makeup is approximately $\frac{3}{5}$ oxygen, $\frac{1}{4}$ carbon, and $\frac{1}{10}$ hydrogen. The rest consists of small amounts of various other elements.
- Our bodies are made up of about 70% water by volume and by weight.
- Although there is a large variation in growth, an average-sized sixth grader weighs about 85 pounds. That's his or her **mass**.
- If we could fill an average-sized sixth grader up with liquid like a big container, he or she would hold about 40.4 quarts. That's his or her **volume**.

## Solve each problem. Use the above information as needed.

1. What fraction of the body is made up of oxygen or hydrogen?

2. How much more of the body is made up of oxygen than carbon?

3. What fraction of the body is made up of oxygen, carbon, and hydrogen together?

4. What fraction of the body is made up elements that are not oxygen, carbon, or hydrogen?

5. How many pounds of water mass make up the average-sized sixth grader?

6. How many quarts of water does an average sixth grader's body contain?

7. $\frac{9}{20}$ of your body is made up of red and white blood cells. 43% of your body is made up of only red blood cells. What fraction of your body is made up of only white blood cells?

8. Blood makes up about 8% of our body weight. How many pounds of a sixth-grader's body mass is made up of blood?

9. The human body gets energy from food. This energy is measured in calories. If a person burns 4.8 calories per minute while walking, how many calories would that person burn during a 20-minute walk?

**Page 5**
1. 7 14 11 12 10 15 15
2. 17 8 12 4 19 5 8
3. 18 11 10 15 12 16 6
4. 12 8 14 12 16 9 17
5. 9 9 13 15 14 13 14
6. 13 18 13 11 11 14 6
7. 12 16 13 12 16 11 13
8. 10 7 10 11 12 17 10

**Page 6**
1. 10 17 12 10 7 10 16
2. 12 13 12 16 6 14 11
3. 13 18 14 13 14 15 13
4. 6 18 9 12 16 9 12
5. 8 14 11 11 9 5 19
6. 8 13 17 15 15 10 11
7. 17 7 10 11 15 11 13
8. 10 9 9 9 14 8 12
9. 17 13 8 4 11 16 14
10. 15 18 12 12 11 8 7

**Page 7**
1. 9 3 9 7 9 4 8
2. 9 8 7 8 4 5 3
3. 4 4 7 6 6 6 2
4. 7 7 7 8 9 6 9
5. 10 7 5 6 1 5 10
6. 2 3 5 3 10 1 3
7. 5 8 3 5 6 8 10
8. 9 6 4 2 9 2 4

**Page 8**
1. 2 2 6 4 7 2 5
2. 2 4 7 10 9 7 3
3. 1 4 6 8 3 7 6
4. 9 6 7 8 2 3 5
5. 7 10 7 5 4 8 10
6. 6 8 1 8 3 1 9
7. 6 6 7 9 5 8 10
8. 5 9 3 4 9 6 2
9. 4 8 5 9 5 3 10
10. 4 5 9 7 6 4 8

**Page 9**
1. 24 3 63 24 49 40 42
2. 6 54 20 36 36 72 45
3. 64 10 4 24 45 21 48
4. 28 35 4 5 28 72 18
5. 56 12 25 8 54 32 15
6. 81 6 63 30 14 7 36
7. 30 32 35 16 9 12 8
8. 9 48 27 56 16 40 18

**Page 10**
1. 9 4 12 30 35 48 5
2. 21 20 48 18 8 18 56
3. 12 36 7 54 10 32 63
4. 36 15 72 56 32 18 40
5. 6 42 20 24 40 9 35
6. 18 16 72 42 16 24 21

7. 3 54 27 12 36 2 81
8. 8 63 15 14 28 14 30
9. 24 28 45 6 64 45 16
10. 25 24 12 49 10 4 27

**Page 11**
1. 9 5 9 8 6 8 2
2. 6 8 1 4 7 3 6
3. 3 5 7 5 2 9 5
4. 7 8 6 4 5 4 4
5. 4 3 2 9 7 9 6
6. 8 6 7 4 8 3 9
7. 2 1 9 3 6 8 5
8. 4 2 8 7 1 5 6

**Page 12**
1. 5 6 8 1 9 9 6
2. 3 4 7 2 4 6 5
3. 2 5 3 9 8 4 9
4. 7 6 2 6 7 8 7
5. 2 8 8 4 2 5 8
6. 4 9 7 2 4 3 2
7. 3 8 6 9 3 3 8
8. 3 6 5 5 1 3 8
9. 6 7 2 6 5 9 7
10. 4 9 1 9 5 4 7

**Page 15**
1. 850 485 454 5,009 9,741
2. 423 5,971 814 1,791 3,712
3. 4,806 25,245 28,512 112,294 483,174
4. 1,366 1,709 6,552 1,628 1,623
5. 78,702 31,577 21,757 1,253,744 715,413
6. c = 112 k = 19 j = 23 n = 187
7. **a.** 10,533 people **b.** 85,711 people
8. 1,781 people

**Page 16**
1. 67 776 1,164 553 1,446 550
2. 794 982 1,262 1,516 535 8,967
3. 2,119 4,643 4,339 16,519 5,691 13,903
4. 11,601 10,062 10,756 7,959 10,322 7,983
5. 66,344 109,018 42,402 82,780 96,057 522,229
6. 117,142 59,429 33,171 74,171 71,391 807,121

**Page 17**
1. 143 108 978 664 1,073 958
2. 576 838 992 1,133 1,779 1,270
3. 4,808 5,741 6,891 10,608 4,976 8,624
4. 7,556 10,244 10,728 14,090 17,514 23,273
5. 142,272 115,246 87,254 146,240 266,201 120,546

**Page 18**
1. 123 222 314 65 614 349
2. 401 81 188 387 397 132
3. 131 148 246 60 432 93
4. 7,273 4,121 1,900 1,058 437 6,989
5. 8,530 4,629 7,801 1,289 1,491 3,095
6. 695 2,893 588 20,356 43,479 428,593

**Page 19**
1. subtract   34,695 people
2. add   3,485,157 people
3. both   2,529,202 people
4. subtract   63 feet
5. subtract   136 feet
6. add   3,807 feet

**Page 20**

|  |  |  |  |  |  |
|---|---|---|---|---|---|
| 1. | 176 | 2,032 | 164 | 2,709 | 3,551 | 1,624 |
| 2. | 5,283 | 1,749 | 5,001 | 3,580 | 3,923 | 4,406 |
| 3. | 6,705 | 2,532 | 3,702 | 506 | 5,511 | 777 |
| 4. | 77,841 | 56,154 | 32,418 | 87,568 | 74,168 | 28,452 |
| 5. | 24,028 | 59,579 | 345,439 | 201,057 | 631,842 | 475,948 |
| 6. | 372,236 | 771,172 | 90,001 | 192,853 | 671,718 | 533,334 |

**Page 21**
1. 122,112
2. 97,349
3. 90,190
4. 86,439
5. 68,655
6. 83,280
7. 131,131
8. 117,473
9. 99,970
10. 103,401
   Total: 1,000,000

**Page 22**
1. subtraction   383 books
2. subtraction   5,692 books
3. addition   6,750 books
4. addition   8,250 books
5. subtraction   17 books
6. subtraction   84 years

**Page 23**
1. $6; z = 8$   $7; a = 11$   $6; z = 8$
2. $7; j = 8$   $5; k = 15$   $7; p = 9$
3. $y = 3$   $x = 16$   $v = 10$   $m = 6$
4. $c = 6$   $n = 12$   $h = 18$   $s = 16$
5. $a = 13$   $w = 9$   $g = 16$   $p = 18$

**Page 24**
1. $6; x = 11$   $8; n = 15$   $8; y = 21$
2. $25; h = 42$   $62; k = 187$   $20; p = 120$
3. $g = 56$   $x = 36$   $j = 26$   $m = 28$
4. $q = 115$   $r = 56$   $w = 64$   $z = 41$
5. $y = 167$   $h = 25$   $a = 36$   $c = 107$
6. $j = 71$   $f = 51$   $d = 122$   $n = 42$

**Page 25**

|  |  |  |  |  |  |
|---|---|---|---|---|---|
| 1. | 242 | 733 | 7,586 | 8,925 | 9,011 |
| 2. | 455 | 853 | 588 | 6,309 | 1,154 |
| 3. | 15,464 | 37,707 | 163,864 | 1,093,718 | 177,974 |
| 4. | 5,458 | 35,788 | 53,528 | 33,890 | 375,649 |

5. $y = 9$   $x = 187$   $k = 15$   $y = 42$
6. a. 55,473 games   b. 1,195,947 computer games
7. 7,585 hits

**Page 26**
1. 1 ft.   38 in.   1 ft 7 in.
2. 56 in.   2 ft.   7 ft.
3. 6 yd.   26 in.   5 ft.
4. 110 in.   1 mi.   11,000 ft.
5. 3 mi.   4 mi.   2 mi.
6. 72 in.   2 yd.   3,520 yd.

**Page 27**
1. fl. oz.   qt.   fl. oz.
2. gal.   c
3. 2 pt.   4 c   1 pt.
4. 16 fl. oz.   12 qt.   16 fl. oz.
5. 8 c   4 p.   2 qt.
6. 6 pt.   $\frac{1}{2}$ gal.   128 fl. oz.
7. 32 qt.   3 gal.   11 qt.
8. >   <   <
9. =   >   <
10. =   >   <

**Page 28**
1. 6 lbs.   48 oz.   14,000 lbs.
2. 32,000 oz.   10 lbs.   5 tons
3. 261 oz.   147 oz.   5,000 lbs.
4. <   <   <
5. =   >   <
6. >   >   <
7. =   =   =
8. 25 ft.
9. 7 qt.
10. 50 lbs.

**Page 29**

|  |  |  |  |  |  |
|---|---|---|---|---|---|
| 1. | 553 | 1,705 | 294 | 14,573 | 12,594 |
| 2. | 35,376 | 154,361 | 36,014 | 705,200 | 4,688,688 |
| 3. | 9 | 16 | 91 | 1,419 | |
| 4. | 68 R47 | 210 R24 | 57 R51 | 406 R52 | |

5. $z = 9$   $x = 512$   $k = 36$   $y = 625$
6. 3,276 miles
7. 9 blankets   8 feet

**Page 30**

|  |  |  |  |  |  |
|---|---|---|---|---|---|
| 1. | 425 | 360 | 116 | 147 | 434 |
| 2. | 4,581 | 844 | 1,680 | 5,598 | 2,505 |
| 3. | 2,896 | 4,205 | 1,611 | 4,314 | 5,679 |
| 4. | 76,342 | 40,502 | 28,935 | 57,202 | 39,132 |
| 5. | 22,050 | 52,290 | 24,305 | 27,849 | 60,298 |
| 6. | 137,620 | 256,236 | 237,402 | 193,672 | 605,032 |

**Page 31**

|  |  |  |  |  |  |
|---|---|---|---|---|---|
| 1. | 1,850 | 1,888 | 2,304 | 3,416 | 1,092 |
| 2. | 2,112 | 4,902 | 5,952 | 2,808 | 3,230 |
| 3. | 23,825 | 16,872 | 16,568 | 39,704 | 16,974 |
| 4. | 76,342 | 61,866 | 34,992 | 61,855 | 40,768 |
| 5. | 205,179 | 289,902 | 157,534 | 617,768 | 391,902 |
| 6. | 835,635 | 84,084 | 115,556 | 253,308 | 296,818 |

**Page 32**

|  |  |  |  |  |  |
|---|---|---|---|---|---|
| 1. | 290,322 | 372,723 | 572,286 | 856,304 | 260,766 |
| 2. | 82,369 | 332,762 | 136,125 | 236,572 | 171,720 |
| 3. | 39,449 | 157,320 | 380,328 | 315,864 | 750,339 |
| 4. | 1,101,790 | 1,210,808 | 480,075 | 385,985 | 547,328 |
| 5. | 544,887 | 1,194,132 | 1,028,526 | 281,352 | 795,918 |
| 6. | 1,667,493 | 1,522,154 | 4,022,856 | 3,352,230 | 958,104 |

# Answer Pages

**Page 33**
1. 214 R1    214 R1    112 R2    113 R4    201 R2
2. 211 R4    270 R4    913 R1    512 R2    708 R2
3. 311 R7    712 R1    650 R1    867    422

**Page 34**
1. 18 R29    22 R19    260 R9    31 R23
2. 222 R8    252 R3    42 R3    122 R61
3. 96 R7    50 R47    2,333 R1    2,025 R43

**Page 35**
1. 6    8    7    4 R408
2. 70 R101    7 R6    34 R73    273 R89
3. 309 R10    501 R18    274 R160    400 R78

**Page 36**
Just fine, tanks.
Worse dis year.
Classy.

**S** = 1,944     **D** = 28,288     **T** = 98 R42
**O** = 104 R2     **W** = 6 R52     **N** = 61,318
**E** = 57,762     **J** = 138,788     **C** = 2,376 R9
**Y** = 4 R1     **U** = 453 R2     **R** = 209,746
**K** = 1,484     **F** = 5,844     **I** = 103 R209
**A** = 61 R4     **L** = 10,080

**Page 37**
1. 8; $t = 9$    9; $n = 9$    6; $y = 7$
2. 7; $z = 5$    5; $h = 10$    7; $k = 8$
3. $x = 4$    $v = 4$    $h = 8$    $g = 3$
4. $n = 8$    $j = 2$    $t = 5$    $d = 10$
5. $b = 4$    $f = 17$    $c = 12$    $r = 13$

**Page 38**
1. 9; $x = 36$    8; $f = 56$    4; $y = 64$
2. 18; $v = 450$    16; $n = 384$    12; $k = 180$
3. $b = 49$    $p = 24$    $t = 63$    $j = 42$
4. $c = 50$    $g = 36$    $y = 1,875$    $s = 242$
5. $w = 918$    $k = 540$    $d = 492$    $z = 464$

**Page 39**
1. 128 people    2. 10 times
3. 40 minutes    4. 8 minutes less
5. 34,000 qt.    6. 30,000 lb.

**Page 40**
1. **a.** 1,300 qt. **b.** 325 gal.    2. 9 years
3. 6 gal.    4. 180 small bags
5. **a.** 14 trucks **b.** 15 tubs    6. 3 boxes

**Page 41**
1. 148    2,490    43,902    9,394
2. 33,628    91,874    221,714    111,606
3. 9    92    4 R3    120 R5
4. 903 R2    3 R9    306 R7    86 R 96
5. $z = 5$    $x = 120$    $k = 17$    $y = 731$
6. $93,080
7. 110 marbles    10. 7 marbles

**Page 42**
1. 11 cm    107 mm
2. 14 cm    144 mm
3. 16 cm    162 mm
4. 8 cm    81 mm
5. 13 cm    127 mm
6. 700 cm    60 dm    35 m
7. 820 cm    8000 m    19 km

**Page 43**
1. $\frac{2}{5}$    $\frac{3}{5}$    $\frac{5}{5}$
2. $\frac{12}{16}$    $\frac{3}{4}$    $\frac{21}{28}$    $\frac{30}{40}$
3. 11    7    6    10
4. $\frac{2}{3}$    $\frac{3}{10}$    $\frac{2}{9}$
5. 20    36    36    15
6. 8    15    24
7. 9    20    30
8. >    >    >
9. $\frac{5}{6}$

**Page 44**
2. $\frac{1}{10}$    $\frac{2}{5}$    $\frac{5}{10}$    $\frac{3}{5}$    $\frac{9}{10}$
3. $\frac{2}{12}$    $\frac{4}{12}$    $\frac{2}{3}$    $\frac{9}{12}$    $\frac{12}{12}$
4. $\frac{2}{16}$    $\frac{2}{8}$    $\frac{8}{16}$    $\frac{5}{8}$    $\frac{14}{16}$

**Page 45 (1–4, answers will vary.)**
1. $\frac{1}{2}$ $\frac{4}{8}$    $\frac{1}{6}$ $\frac{4}{24}$    $\frac{4}{7}$ $\frac{16}{28}$    $\frac{2}{9}$ $\frac{8}{36}$
2. $\frac{5}{12}$ $\frac{20}{48}$    $\frac{8}{18}$ $\frac{16}{36}$    $\frac{1}{2}$ $\frac{5}{10}$ $\frac{20}{40}$    $\frac{3}{4}$ $\frac{6}{8}$
3. $\frac{1}{8}$ $\frac{4}{32}$    $\frac{5}{6}$ $\frac{20}{24}$    $\frac{16}{18}$ $\frac{24}{27}$    $\frac{2}{5}$ $\frac{8}{20}$
4. $\frac{1}{8}$ $\frac{4}{32}$    $\frac{6}{20}$ $\frac{9}{30}$    $\frac{14}{36}$ $\frac{21}{54}$    $\frac{9}{20}$ $\frac{36}{80}$
5. 3    80    8
6. 9    60    15
7. 6    36    90
8. 66    20    120

**Page 46**
1. 6: 1, 2, 3, 6    4: 1, 2, 4
   18: 1, 2, 3, 6, 9, 18    12: 1, 2, 3, 4, 6, 12
   GCF 6    GCF 4
2. 12: 1, 2, 3, 4, 6, 12    14: 1, 2, 7, 14
   18: 1, 2, 3, 6, 9, 18    21: 1, 3, 7, 21
   GCF 6    GCF 7
3. 18: 1, 2, 3, 6, 9, 18    24: 1, 2, 3, 4, 6, 8, 12
   27: 1, 3, 9, 27    32: 1, 2, 4, 8, 16, 32
   GCF 9    GCF 8
4. 9: 1, 3, 9    9: 1, 3, 9
   12: 1, 2, 3, 4, 6, 12    15: 1, 3, 5, 15
   GCF 3    GCF 3
5. 15: 1, 3, 5, 15    15: 1, 3, 5, 15
   20: 1, 2, 4, 5, 10, 20    40: 1, 2, 4, 5, 8, 10, 20, 40
   GCF 5    GCF 5
6. 14: 1, 2, 7, 14    15: 1, 3, 5, 15
   35: 1, 5, 7, 35    35: 1, 5, 7, 35
   GCF 7    GCF 5

# Answer Pages

## Page 47

1. $\frac{2}{3}$   $\frac{1}{2}$   $\frac{3}{5}$   $\frac{4}{7}$   $\frac{2}{15}$
2. $\frac{1}{9}$   $\frac{5}{18}$   $\frac{5}{6}$   $\frac{14}{15}$   $\frac{1}{4}$
3. $\frac{2}{7}$   $\frac{2}{3}$   $\frac{11}{15}$   $\frac{15}{32}$   $\frac{7}{10}$
4. $\frac{1}{3}$   $\frac{1}{2}$   $\frac{4}{5}$   $\frac{1}{2}$   $\frac{11}{16}$
5. $\frac{34}{59}$   $\frac{1}{4}$   $\frac{13}{14}$   $\frac{1}{5}$   $\frac{15}{16}$
6. $\frac{3}{5}$   $\frac{1}{5}$   $\frac{1}{3}$   $\frac{3}{10}$   $\frac{2}{15}$

## Page 48

1. LCM 6    LCM 8
2. LCM 15    LCM 12
3. LCM 24    LCM 30
4. LCM 60    LCM 30
5. LCM 30    LCM 36
6. LCM 40    LCM 30

## Page 49

1. $\frac{1}{9}$ $\frac{3}{9}$   $\frac{2}{6}$ $\frac{1}{6}$   $\frac{25}{30}$ $\frac{12}{30}$
2. $\frac{12}{24}$ $\frac{16}{24}$   $\frac{6}{18}$ $\frac{6}{18}$   $\frac{36}{45}$ $\frac{15}{45}$
3. $\frac{14}{28}$ $\frac{12}{28}$   $\frac{16}{24}$ $\frac{18}{24}$   $\frac{18}{30}$ $\frac{25}{30}$
4. $\frac{2}{16}$ $\frac{1}{16}$   $\frac{1}{12}$ $\frac{3}{12}$   $\frac{1}{18}$ $\frac{2}{18}$
5. $\frac{12}{18}$ $\frac{3}{18}$   $\frac{8}{32}$ $\frac{4}{32}$   $\frac{16}{20}$ $\frac{6}{20}$
6. $\frac{9}{36}$ $\frac{6}{36}$   $\frac{24}{56}$ $\frac{21}{56}$   $\frac{11}{22}$ $\frac{8}{22}$

## Page 50

1. $=$   $>$   $>$   $<$
2. $>$   $<$   $>$   $>$
3. $<$   $>$   $=$   $<$
4. $\frac{1}{3}$ $\frac{7}{12}$ $\frac{5}{6}$   $\frac{3}{4}$ $\frac{13}{16}$ $\frac{7}{8}$   $\frac{9}{14}$ $\frac{5}{7}$ $\frac{3}{4}$
5. $\frac{1}{2}$ $\frac{3}{4}$ $\frac{5}{6}$   $\frac{3}{8}$ $\frac{3}{7}$ $\frac{3}{5}$   $\frac{3}{4}$ $\frac{4}{5}$ $\frac{17}{20}$

## Page 51

1. $\frac{4}{5}$
2. $\frac{6}{16}$ or $\frac{3}{8}$ of the pizza
3. 32 pizzas
4. **a.** 12 slices
   **b.** Maria = 4 slices, Ally = 3 slices, Mindy = 3 slices, Bethany = 2 slices
5. **a.** green peppers **b.** mushrooms
6. $\frac{21}{54}$ or $\frac{7}{18}$

## Page 52

1. Shopping, Outdoor Recreation
2. $\frac{3}{16}$ Cultural Events
3. $\frac{3}{4}$ Shopping
4. Outdoor Recreation
5. $\frac{1}{4}$
6. Museums
7. Theme Park

## Page 53

1. $\frac{2}{8}$   $\frac{2}{4}$   $\frac{5}{8}$   $\frac{6}{8}$
2. $\boxed{\frac{3}{8}}$ $\frac{1}{3}$ $\boxed{\frac{9}{24}}$ $\frac{6}{24}$ $\boxed{\frac{12}{32}}$ $\frac{18}{36}$
3. 5   5   6   20
4. $\frac{3}{4}$   $\frac{7}{8}$   $\frac{1}{3}$
5. 60   60   28   35
6. $\frac{3}{9}$ $\frac{7}{9}$   $\frac{12}{20}$ $\frac{10}{20}$   $\frac{8}{20}$ $\frac{15}{20}$
7. $\frac{3}{8}$ $\frac{4}{8}$   $\frac{10}{15}$ $\frac{12}{15}$   $\frac{18}{30}$ $\frac{16}{30}$
8. $>$   $<$   $>$
9. $\frac{7}{12}$

## Page 54

1. $\frac{7}{18}$   $\frac{4}{9}$
2. $\frac{5}{6}$   $\frac{5}{9}$   $\frac{5}{9}$
3. $\frac{11}{18}$   $\frac{11}{18}$   1
4. $\frac{1}{8}$   $\frac{1}{4}$
5. $\frac{1}{2}$   $\frac{3}{4}$   $\frac{5}{8}$
6. $\frac{1}{6}$   $\frac{1}{3}$   $\frac{1}{2}$
7. $\frac{5}{6}$   $\frac{1}{2}$   $\frac{2}{3}$

## Page 55

1. $\frac{7}{3}$   $\frac{35}{5}$   $\frac{33}{5}$   $\frac{71}{6}$
2. $3\frac{2}{7}$   $6\frac{1}{2}$   7   $5\frac{5}{16}$
3. $\frac{4}{5}$   $1\frac{1}{4}$   $1\frac{1}{15}$   $\frac{13}{18}$
4. $\frac{2}{3}$   $\frac{7}{12}$   $\frac{7}{60}$   $\frac{1}{9}$
5. 11   $5\frac{1}{10}$   $14\frac{3}{8}$   $16\frac{9}{20}$
6. $2\frac{3}{4}$   $5\frac{2}{9}$   $4\frac{5}{12}$   $5\frac{5}{42}$
7. $4\frac{1}{4}$ hours
8. $2\frac{3}{16}$ inches

## Page 56

1. $1\frac{1}{3}$   $2\frac{1}{2}$   5   $1\frac{5}{12}$   $8\frac{2}{3}$
2. $3\frac{1}{3}$   9   $3\frac{4}{13}$   $6\frac{1}{5}$   $6\frac{2}{3}$
3. $9\frac{1}{3}$   $6\frac{3}{8}$   $6\frac{2}{3}$   5   $6\frac{5}{8}$
4. 5   $8\frac{1}{2}$   $7\frac{3}{5}$   $5\frac{2}{5}$   $3\frac{2}{3}$

## Page 57

1. $\frac{26}{3}$   $\frac{27}{5}$   $\frac{5}{2}$   $\frac{35}{8}$
2. $\frac{27}{4}$   $\frac{24}{5}$   $\frac{32}{3}$   $\frac{51}{4}$
3. $\frac{52}{5}$   $\frac{122}{11}$   $\frac{23}{16}$   $\frac{26}{3}$
4. $\frac{41}{6}$   $\frac{29}{8}$   $\frac{81}{16}$   $\frac{151}{12}$
5. 5   12   8   24
6. 24   30   60   32
7. 54   55   26   75

## Page 58

1. $\frac{1}{7}$   1   $\frac{1}{2}$
2. $1\frac{2}{3}$   $\frac{2}{3}$   $1\frac{1}{5}$
3. $\frac{7}{20}$   $\frac{6}{11}$   $\frac{1}{2}$
4. $1\frac{1}{3}$   $1\frac{2}{5}$   $\frac{2}{3}$   $\frac{2}{9}$   $\frac{1}{2}$
5. $\frac{3}{5}$   $1\frac{3}{7}$   $\frac{1}{4}$   $1\frac{1}{3}$   $\frac{1}{2}$

# Answer Pages

**Page 59**
1. $5$ | $4\frac{2}{5}$ | $4\frac{2}{3}$ | $6$ | $1\frac{1}{3}$
2. $9$ | $1\frac{2}{3}$ | $2$ | $1\frac{1}{2}$ | $10\frac{2}{5}$
3. $2\frac{3}{8}$ | $7\frac{1}{2}$ | $3\frac{4}{7}$ | $15\frac{2}{3}$ | $3\frac{4}{7}$
4. $1\frac{5}{12}$ | $2\frac{2}{3}$ | $3$ | $1\frac{1}{3}$ | $9\frac{3}{5}$
5. $6\frac{3}{10}$ | $4\frac{1}{8}$ | $7\frac{3}{5}$ | $7$ | $2\frac{1}{2}$

**Page 60**
1. $5$ | $1\frac{3}{4}$ | $2\frac{1}{3}$ | $3\frac{1}{2}$ | $5\frac{4}{5}$
2. $2\frac{5}{7}$ | $1\frac{4}{5}$ | $4\frac{3}{5}$ | $5\frac{3}{4}$ | $6\frac{7}{8}$
3. $5\frac{3}{4}$ | $4\frac{1}{2}$ | $2\frac{1}{4}$ | $2\frac{1}{8}$ | $4\frac{4}{5}$
4. $6\frac{1}{3}$ | $\frac{4}{5}$ | $2\frac{1}{4}$ | $11\frac{7}{9}$ | $13\frac{5}{9}$
5. $3\frac{3}{5}$ | $3\frac{11}{15}$ | $3\frac{9}{16}$ | $5\frac{2}{3}$ | $5\frac{13}{18}$

**Page 61**
1. $4\frac{2}{5}$ | $4\frac{7}{8}$ | $5\frac{4}{9}$
2. $2\frac{4}{5}$ | $\frac{1}{2}$ | $2\frac{3}{4}$
3. $3\frac{3}{4}$ | $3\frac{2}{3}$ | $9\frac{2}{3}$
4. $5\frac{4}{5}$ | $6\frac{7}{8}$ | $9\frac{3}{5}$

**Page 62**
1. $\frac{11}{12}$ | $\frac{7}{18}$ | $1\frac{1}{10}$ | $\frac{7}{20}$ | $1\frac{1}{9}$
2. $1\frac{5}{24}$ | $1\frac{3}{8}$ | $\frac{1}{15}$ | $1\frac{1}{20}$ | $\frac{29}{42}$
3. $\frac{1}{5}$ | $1\frac{3}{10}$ | $\frac{2}{15}$ | $1\frac{5}{21}$ | $\frac{37}{40}$
4. $\frac{1}{12}$ | $\frac{3}{10}$ | $\frac{1}{6}$ | $1\frac{5}{21}$ | $\frac{16}{35}$
5. $\frac{1}{3}$ | $\frac{1}{16}$ | $\frac{3}{5}$ | $\frac{13}{15}$ | $\frac{1}{16}$

**Page 63**
1. $7\frac{3}{5}$ | $13\frac{5}{12}$ | $9\frac{5}{8}$ | $17\frac{7}{20}$ | $3\frac{11}{12}$
2. $6\frac{13}{24}$ | $11\frac{1}{5}$ | $6\frac{2}{3}$ | $4\frac{1}{3}$ | $3\frac{5}{12}$
3. $19\frac{5}{24}$ | $14\frac{17}{24}$ | $13\frac{7}{20}$ | $28\frac{3}{8}$ | $25\frac{7}{12}$
4. $3\frac{5}{24}$ | $4\frac{7}{20}$ | $2\frac{1}{6}$ | $3\frac{7}{20}$ | $5\frac{1}{24}$
5. $36\frac{7}{15}$ | $15\frac{13}{14}$ | $15\frac{7}{36}$ | $15\frac{25}{36}$ | $31\frac{5}{6}$
6. $4\frac{20}{21}$ | $3\frac{1}{3}$ | $11\frac{1}{7}$ | $13\frac{1}{12}$ | $4\frac{2}{5}$

**Page 64**
1. $1\frac{13}{16}$ | $3\frac{5}{7}$ | $5\frac{11}{15}$ | $3\frac{1}{2}$
2. $3\frac{5}{9}$ | $1\frac{3}{10}$ | $\frac{5}{16}$ | $3\frac{13}{20}$
3. $14\frac{5}{6}$ | $12\frac{7}{8}$ | $12\frac{11}{15}$ | $3\frac{25}{42}$
4. $11\frac{3}{10}$ | $4\frac{2}{5}$ | $11\frac{11}{16}$ | $4\frac{3}{5}$
5. $8\frac{1}{4}$ | $8\frac{3}{4}$ | $\frac{4}{5}$ | $10\frac{5}{16}$

**Page 65**
K $\frac{1}{2}$ | D $\frac{1}{8}$ | L $2\frac{2}{3}$ | O $7\frac{1}{15}$
R $8\frac{3}{7}$ | A $7\frac{1}{6}$ | F $3\frac{1}{4}$ | H $4\frac{4}{9}$
B $1\frac{4}{5}$ | M $3\frac{1}{2}$ | C $2\frac{5}{6}$ | N $6\frac{3}{4}$
S $\frac{2}{9}$ | F $\frac{1}{20}$ | G $\frac{1}{15}$ | E $\frac{3}{8}$
T $1\frac{2}{3}$ | L $4\frac{13}{20}$ | I $\frac{4}{5}$ | P $7\frac{1}{2}$
A case of blackmail

**Page 66**
1. $\frac{1}{10}$ | $2\frac{3}{10}$ | $\frac{7}{10}$ | $\frac{2}{5}$
2. $\frac{1}{5}$ | $\frac{3}{5}$ | $\frac{1}{15}$ | $\frac{7}{15}$
3. $1\frac{7}{16}$ | $1\frac{9}{16}$ | $1\frac{5}{16}$ | $1\frac{1}{16}$ | $1\frac{3}{16}$
4. $2\frac{1}{18}$ | $2\frac{7}{18}$ | $2\frac{5}{18}$ | $2\frac{1}{6}$ | $2\frac{1}{2}$

**Page 67**
1. $1\frac{1}{4}$ cups
2. $4$ cups | 3. $\frac{3}{8}$ cups | 4. $4\frac{1}{8}$ cups
5. $5\frac{15}{16}$ miles | 6. $3\frac{3}{5}$ miles

**Page 68**
1. a. $3\frac{1}{3}$ innings b. $2\frac{1}{3}$ innings
2. $2\frac{1}{2}$ games | 3. $\frac{5}{8}$ inches | 4. $\frac{7}{24}$ fans
5. $\frac{19}{24}$ | 6. 6:45 p.m.

**Page 69**
1. $\frac{7}{5}$ | $\frac{23}{4}$ | $\frac{23}{6}$ | $\frac{103}{8}$
2. $5\frac{3}{5}$ | $6\frac{1}{3}$ | $3$ | $4\frac{4}{5}$
3. $\frac{5}{7}$ | $1\frac{1}{3}$ | $1\frac{3}{20}$ | $1\frac{1}{25}$
4. $\frac{3}{7}$ | $\frac{5}{12}$ | $\frac{3}{20}$ | $\frac{17}{45}$
5. $9$ | $8\frac{3}{10}$ | $18\frac{3}{8}$ | $19\frac{19}{24}$
6. $5\frac{2}{5}$ | $3\frac{5}{14}$ | $4\frac{35}{72}$ | $8\frac{7}{9}$
7. $\frac{7}{15}$
8. $1\frac{5}{8}$ inches

**Page 70**
1. 20, 23, 26; 47, 55, 63 | 2. 66, 61, 56; 60, 52, 44
3. 50, 55, 65; 34, 21, 8 | 4. 657, 742, 827; 191,383, 767
5. 172, 154, 136; 36, 49, 64 | 6. 32, 64, 128; 68, 74, 81
7. 60, 74, 90; 55, 44, 33 | 8. 22, 20, 25; 94, 109, 124

**Page 71**
1. $\frac{1}{16}$ | $\frac{1}{40}$ | $\frac{8}{21}$ | $\frac{9}{16}$
2. $\frac{9}{10}$ | $\frac{12}{35}$ | $6$ | $4\frac{2}{3}$
3. $2\frac{1}{2}$ | $2$ | $1\frac{19}{20}$ | $2\frac{2}{9}$
4. $\frac{8}{9}$ | $\frac{5}{8}$ | $7\frac{1}{5}$ | $1\frac{5}{9}$
5. $4\frac{1}{3}$ | $9\frac{3}{4}$ | $14$ | $5$
6. $10\frac{5}{8}$ miles
7. 14 newspapers

**Page 72**
1. $\frac{1}{40}$ | $\frac{1}{28}$ | $\frac{1}{96}$ | $\frac{1}{150}$
2. $\frac{12}{35}$ | $\frac{3}{5}$ | $\frac{8}{21}$ | $\frac{9}{16}$
3. $\frac{2}{3}$ | $\frac{7}{12}$ | $\frac{56}{81}$ | $\frac{3}{5}$
4. $\frac{1}{12}$ | $\frac{2}{9}$ | $\frac{3}{16}$ | $\frac{1}{2}$
5. $\frac{21}{50}$ | $\frac{10}{49}$ | $\frac{4}{9}$ | $\frac{2}{3}$
6. $\frac{9}{28}$ | $\frac{5}{12}$ | $\frac{5}{12}$ | $\frac{2}{7}$

**Page 73**
1. $\frac{1}{3}$ | $2\frac{1}{2}$ | $\frac{1}{2}$ | $1\frac{3}{4}$
2. $1\frac{3}{4}$ | $2\frac{1}{2}$ | $1\frac{1}{2}$ | $3$
3. $2\frac{1}{4}$ | $1\frac{1}{3}$ | $3\frac{1}{3}$ | $4$
4. $1\frac{4}{5}$ | $1$ | $1\frac{1}{2}$ | $1\frac{1}{17}$
5. $\frac{4}{5}$ | $4\frac{1}{6}$ | $2\frac{1}{4}$ | $1\frac{1}{4}$
6. $1\frac{4}{11}$ | $1\frac{1}{6}$ | $1\frac{11}{13}$ | $2\frac{3}{4}$

# Answer Pages

## Page 74
1. $1\frac{1}{12}$  $1\frac{1}{10}$  $1\frac{1}{12}$  $1\frac{2}{5}$
2. $2\frac{3}{8}$  $2\frac{5}{10}$  $\frac{19}{24}$  $\frac{29}{36}$
3. $1\frac{13}{20}$  $3\frac{3}{10}$  $\frac{9}{14}$  $2\frac{1}{6}$
4. $\frac{21}{40}$  $\frac{9}{10}$  $1\frac{2}{5}$  $1\frac{17}{27}$
5. $\frac{5}{8}$  $\frac{1}{4}$  $\frac{1}{2}$  $1\frac{1}{50}$
6. $\frac{27}{44}$  $1\frac{1}{3}$  $\frac{13}{30}$  $\frac{3}{25}$

## Page 75
1. $13\frac{5}{12}$  $2\frac{17}{30}$  $5\frac{5}{8}$  $4\frac{2}{3}$
2. $2\frac{1}{2}$  $4\frac{41}{64}$  $13\frac{1}{8}$  $3\frac{1}{9}$
3. $4\frac{1}{4}$  $4\frac{1}{12}$  $8\frac{13}{15}$  $1\frac{2}{3}$
4. $4\frac{7}{8}$  $5\frac{13}{28}$  $3\frac{3}{35}$  $3\frac{23}{24}$
5. $9\frac{1}{10}$  $1\frac{43}{45}$  $2\frac{25}{64}$  $3\frac{3}{10}$
6. $3\frac{3}{7}$  $4\frac{1}{5}$  $1\frac{4}{9}$  $1\frac{4}{5}$

## Page 76
1. $14$  $15\frac{2}{5}$  $7\frac{4}{5}$  $11\frac{5}{9}$
2. $2\frac{3}{4}$  $22\frac{1}{2}$  $16\frac{4}{5}$  $5\frac{1}{7}$
3. $7$  $5\frac{5}{8}$  $7\frac{1}{2}$  $8\frac{4}{5}$
4. $6\frac{6}{7}$  $8\frac{2}{5}$  $11$  $6\frac{1}{4}$
5. $6\frac{2}{3}$  $3\frac{1}{4}$  $14\frac{2}{5}$  $26\frac{1}{4}$
6. $25\frac{3}{5}$  $3\frac{6}{7}$  $16$  $7\frac{1}{2}$

## Page 77
1. $4$  $20$  $48$  $33$
2. $56$  $30$  $60$  $84$
3. $7\frac{1}{2}$  $21\frac{1}{3}$  $58\frac{1}{2}$  $9\frac{1}{4}$
4. $12\frac{1}{2}$  $7\frac{1}{3}$  $8\frac{1}{3}$  $31\frac{1}{2}$
5. 16 students are girls
6. 72 cookies
7. 190 students

## Page 78
1. $\frac{1}{6}$  2. $5$  3. $\frac{3}{20}$  4. $\frac{1}{2}$
5. $\frac{1}{3}$  6. $6\frac{5}{6}$  7. $2\frac{2}{3}$  8. $4$
9. $4\frac{1}{2}$  10. $11\frac{11}{20}$  11. $6\frac{6}{7}$  12. $11\frac{1}{5}$
13. $\frac{7}{18}$  14. $\frac{1}{60}$  15. $8\frac{17}{18}$  16. $\frac{8}{21}$
17. $\frac{1}{20}$  18. $1\frac{1}{5}$  19. $\frac{15}{32}$  20. $4\frac{4}{15}$

START -- $5$ -- $\frac{3}{20}$ -- $\frac{1}{2}$ -- $\frac{1}{3}$ -- $6\frac{5}{6}$ -- $2\frac{2}{3}$ -- $4$ -- $4\frac{1}{2}$ -- $11\frac{11}{20}$ --
$6\frac{6}{7}$ -- $11\frac{1}{5}$ -- $\frac{7}{18}$ -- $\frac{1}{60}$ -- $8\frac{17}{18}$ -- $\frac{8}{21}$ -- $\frac{1}{20}$ -- $1\frac{1}{5}$ -- $\frac{15}{32}$ -- $4\frac{4}{15}$ --
FINISH

## Page 79
RON DE VOO
IMA SHARK
LYLE OTT
AMOS KEETAH

A $\frac{2}{9}$  B $\frac{21}{52}$  C $\frac{3}{11}$  D $\frac{16}{91}$
E $\frac{1}{18}$  F $\frac{1}{13}$  G $1\frac{1}{2}$  H $\frac{7}{9}$
I $4\frac{5}{16}$  J $1\frac{5}{27}$  K $2\frac{5}{8}$  L $10\frac{5}{16}$
M $\frac{1}{3}$  N $\frac{1}{2}$  O $\frac{3}{4}$  P $\frac{4}{11}$
Q $\frac{2}{11}$  R $\frac{10}{21}$  S $1\frac{5}{9}$  T $\frac{9}{14}$
U $24\frac{4}{9}$  V $\frac{5}{26}$  W $3\frac{3}{20}$  X $3\frac{1}{5}$
Y $\frac{13}{18}$  Z $2\frac{3}{7}$

## Page 80
1. $1\frac{1}{6}$ cups  2. $5\frac{1}{4}$ tsp chile powder , $2\frac{1}{4}$ tbsp olive oil
3. 14, 2 ounces  4. $1\frac{1}{3}$
5. $1\frac{7}{9}$ cups  6. 2 cups
7. 401°F

## Page 81
1. $\frac{4}{9}$

## Page 82
1. $\frac{1}{4}$ meter  2. $5\frac{3}{25}$ meters
3. Month 5  4. 8 minutes
5. 400 birds  6. 400

## Page 83
1. $\frac{2}{15}$  $\frac{4}{21}$  $\frac{5}{21}$  $\frac{5}{14}$
2. $\frac{2}{3}$  $\frac{1}{2}$  $\frac{8}{13}$  $\frac{8}{11}$
3. $\frac{9}{16}$  $3\frac{1}{3}$  $1\frac{11}{24}$  $3\frac{43}{64}$
4. $1\frac{1}{9}$  $\frac{3}{10}$  $1\frac{1}{3}$  $3\frac{5}{9}$
5. $13\frac{1}{8}$  $8\frac{8}{11}$  $12\frac{3}{8}$  $3\frac{1}{2}$
6. $6\frac{3}{8}$ yards
7. $1\frac{11}{16}$

## Page 84
1. $\frac{3}{2}$ or $1\frac{1}{2}$  $\frac{4}{7}$  $\frac{2}{9}$  $\frac{1}{5}$  $\frac{3}{34}$
2. $24$  $24$  $30$  $5\frac{1}{3}$
3. $7$  $6\frac{2}{3}$  $\frac{15}{16}$  $1$
4. $\frac{10}{21}$  $5\frac{1}{3}$  $2\frac{3}{4}$  $4\frac{2}{3}$
5. $\frac{1}{8}$  $\frac{3}{16}$  $\frac{9}{20}$  $\frac{26}{45}$
6. $1\frac{5}{8}$  $1\frac{2}{3}$  $4\frac{4}{5}$  $1\frac{7}{26}$
7. $n = 1\frac{5}{6}$  $n = 1\frac{1}{48}$
8. $n = 4\frac{2}{5}$  $n = 3\frac{1}{16}$
9. 10 beads

## Page 85
1. $\frac{5}{11}$  $\frac{4}{9}$  $\frac{1}{9}$  $3\frac{1}{3}$  $\frac{3}{26}$
2. $7$  $\frac{8}{37}$  $\frac{11}{15}$  $6$  $\frac{2}{9}$
3. $1\frac{1}{3}$  $\frac{1}{3}$  $\frac{4}{9}$  $\frac{8}{61}$  $1$
4. $\frac{3}{17}$  $1\frac{2}{7}$  $\frac{1}{27}$  $\frac{5}{11}$  $\frac{5}{17}$
5. $3$  $\frac{1}{22}$  $\frac{7}{10}$  $\frac{8}{17}$  $\frac{8}{79}$

## Page 86
1. $7, 7$  $2, 2$  $2, 2$
2. $13\frac{1}{2}, 13\frac{1}{2}$  $6\frac{2}{3}, 6\frac{2}{3}$  $8\frac{3}{4}, 8\frac{3}{4}$
3. $1\frac{1}{2}$  $\frac{1}{2}$  $\frac{3}{10}$  $\frac{3}{5}$
4. $5$  $2$  $\frac{5}{6}$  $\frac{3}{5}$
5. $2\frac{1}{2}$  $1\frac{11}{24}$  $1\frac{1}{6}$  $1\frac{1}{7}$
6. $\frac{11}{15}$  $\frac{1}{4}$  $1\frac{1}{3}$  $1\frac{5}{9}$
7. $24\frac{1}{2}$  $4\frac{1}{2}$  $1\frac{2}{3}$  $3\frac{1}{3}$

# Answer Pages

**Page 87**
1. $13\frac{1}{2}$    35    $\frac{1}{14}$    $\frac{3}{5}$
2. $\frac{3}{20}$    $\frac{1}{8}$    $\frac{9}{40}$    $\frac{1}{18}$
3. $\frac{3}{8}$    $\frac{5}{12}$    $\frac{4}{15}$    $\frac{8}{25}$
4. $\frac{5}{18}$    $\frac{7}{12}$    12    $12\frac{1}{2}$

**Page 88**
1. 4    $1\frac{3}{4}$    $1\frac{9}{25}$    $1\frac{3}{4}$
2. $\frac{3}{4}$    2    $3\frac{1}{6}$    $1\frac{2}{7}$
3. $6\frac{2}{3}$    $4\frac{1}{2}$    $1\frac{1}{5}$    $\frac{23}{26}$
4. $3\frac{3}{7}$    3    $\frac{1}{2}$    $3\frac{3}{8}$
5. 2    3    $\frac{5}{6}$    $\frac{33}{68}$
6. $\frac{39}{50}$    $1\frac{3}{32}$    $4\frac{2}{3}$    $1\frac{1}{4}$

**Page 89**
1. $n = \frac{2}{5}$    $n = \frac{2}{3}$    $n = 2\frac{2}{3}$
2. $n = 1$    $n = \frac{2}{5}$    $n = 2\frac{1}{4}$
3. $n = \frac{1}{3}$    $n = 2\frac{1}{4}$    $n = 13\frac{1}{3}$
4. $n = 2\frac{1}{3}$    $n = 5\frac{1}{3}$    $n = 21$
5. $n = 36\frac{3}{4}$    $n = 25$    $n = 6$

**Page 90**
1. $n = \frac{7}{20}$    $n = 8\frac{1}{3}$    $n = 2\frac{5}{8}$
2. $n = \frac{2}{45}$    $n = 3\frac{3}{5}$    $n = \frac{5}{12}$
3. $n = \frac{1}{24}$    $n = \frac{3}{16}$    $n = 12$
4. $n = 4\frac{2}{3}$    $n = 14\frac{2}{3}$    $n = 8\frac{4}{7}$
5. $n = 18\frac{3}{4}$    $n = 2\frac{5}{8}$    $n = 13\frac{1}{8}$

**Page 91**
Start -- $\frac{1}{2}$ -- $\frac{3}{4}$ -- $\frac{5}{6}$ -- $\frac{1}{2}$ -- $1\frac{1}{3}$ -- $5\frac{1}{3}$ -- $6\frac{2}{5}$ -- 2 -- $1\frac{2}{3}$ -- $2\frac{1}{2}$

**Page 92**
1. $\frac{5}{6}$    1    $6\frac{7}{15}$    $1\frac{1}{3}$
2. $\frac{2}{3}$    $10\frac{1}{2}$    $\frac{1}{3}$    $\frac{1}{3}$
3. $\frac{2}{15}$    $\frac{1}{4}$    $4\frac{19}{24}$    $2\frac{11}{15}$
4. $\frac{1}{18}$    $14\frac{3}{10}$    $3\frac{1}{4}$    $3\frac{11}{12}$
5. $\frac{3}{35}$    24    $3\frac{15}{16}$    $\frac{17}{30}$
6. 28    $2\frac{3}{4}$    $\frac{1}{20}$    $\frac{4}{33}$
7. $3\frac{9}{16}$    3    $1\frac{11}{21}$    $3\frac{5}{9}$
8. $1\frac{41}{63}$    $\frac{4}{13}$    $7\frac{1}{2}$    $4\frac{4}{23}$

**Page 93**
1. 8 servings    2. $6\frac{1}{2}$ ounces
3. $1\frac{3}{4}$ pounds    4. $\frac{3}{20}$ pounds
5. $\frac{11}{12}$ feet or 11 inches    6. $2\frac{1}{3}$ ounces
7. $\frac{11}{36}$ pounds

**Page 94**
1. 198 pounds    2. $75\frac{3}{5}$ pounds
3. $183\frac{1}{3}$ pounds    4. 75 pounds
5. $18\frac{1}{8}$ pounds    6. 57 pounds

**Page 95**
1. $\frac{4}{3}$    $\frac{5}{8}$    $\frac{3}{16}$    $\frac{5}{51}$
2. 8    20    6    6
3. $10\frac{1}{2}$    3    1    $\frac{1}{2}$
4. $\frac{5}{6}$    $1\frac{1}{4}$    $13\frac{1}{2}$    $3\frac{3}{5}$
5. $\frac{3}{16}$    $\frac{7}{18}$    $1\frac{4}{5}$    $\frac{4}{5}$
6. $1\frac{1}{11}$    $\frac{21}{32}$    $\frac{2}{3}$    $1\frac{19}{20}$
7. $n = \frac{21}{50}$    $n = \frac{1}{35}$
8. $n = 2\frac{9}{10}$    $n = 9\frac{5}{27}$
9. 6 runners

**Page 96**
1. $\overleftrightarrow{CD}$ or $\overleftrightarrow{DC}$    $\overrightarrow{KL}$    $\overline{MN}$ or $\overline{NM}$    $\overleftrightarrow{TU}$ or $\overleftrightarrow{UT}$
2. $\overline{RV}$ or $\overline{VR}$    $\overline{EF}$    $\overrightarrow{AZ}$    $\overrightarrow{JI}$ or $\overrightarrow{IJ}$
3. X Y    P Q    G H    Y Z

**Page 97**
1. D    2. G    3. A
4. E    5. I    6. C
7. H    8. F    9. B

**Page 98**
1. $\angle$ABC    $\angle$CBA    $\angle$B    right
   $\angle$MPV    $\angle$VPM    $\angle$P    acute
   $\angle$CJG    $\angle$GJC    $\angle$J    obtuse
   $\angle$AVW    $\angle$WVA    $\angle$V    right
2. $\angle$DMS    $\angle$SMD    $\angle$S    acute
   $\angle$ABR    $\angle$RBA    $\angle$B    obtuse
   $\angle$LMN    $\angle$NML    $\angle$M    right
   $\angle$IKJ    $\angle$JKI    $\angle$K    obtuse

**Page 99**
1. 45°, acute    130°, obtuse    30°, acute
2. 110°, obtuse    65°, acute    90°, right
3. 100°, obtuse    90°, right    40°, acute
4. 155°, obtuse    90°, right    20°, acute

**Page 100**
1. 40°, acute    80°, acute    90°, right    75°, acute
2. 39°, acute    46°, acute    97°, obtuse    90°, right

**Page 101**
1. 13, 19, 29 add 9

**Page 102**
1. 16    40    80    multiply by 4
2. 9    11    19    199    multiply by 2, subtract 1

**Page 103**
1. 11    13    15    $x + 4 = y$
   7    8    9    $x - 2 = y$
2. 24    28    32    $4 \cdot x = y$
   24    30    36    $3 \cdot x = y$
3. 6    7    8    $x \div 2 = y$
   4    9    20    $x - 1 = y$
4. 20    21    22    $x + 15 = y$
   26    28    30    $2 \cdot x = y$

**Page 104**

1. Mean, 36  Median, 34  Mode, 41  Range, 10
   Mean, 16  Median, 13  Mode, 10  Range, 27
2. Mean, $14  Median, $14  Mode, None  Range, $16
   Mean, $49  Median, $41  Mode, $41  Range, $66
3. Mean, 91  Median, 90  Mode, 93  Range, 33

**Page 105**

1. 44 green marbles
2. 540 students
3. 160 students
4. 30 small, 90 medium, 130 large
5. 78 votes

**Page 106**

1. 0.5    0.4    0.3    3.8    4.6
2. 0.50   1.10   0.36   3.32   0.60
3. 4.35   0.50   2.08   0.40   0.96
4. 0.25   6.75   0.80   7.05   0.52
5. 0.375  0.200  5.48   0.625  3.070
6. 0.056  1.012  0.250  8.360  0.448
7. 6.500  0.789  4.160  0.016  2.625

**Page 107**

1. $\frac{1}{10}$    $2\frac{3}{5}$    $\frac{2}{5}$    $6\frac{1}{2}$
2. $8\frac{7}{10}$   $\frac{9}{10}$    $4\frac{4}{5}$   $\frac{3}{10}$
3. $\frac{1}{5}$     $\frac{1}{4}$     $\frac{11}{20}$  $6\frac{17}{50}$
4. $8\frac{2}{25}$   $\frac{1}{25}$    $\frac{1}{100}$  $4\frac{3}{50}$
5. $\frac{21}{50}$   $1\frac{3}{4}$    $\frac{61}{125}$ $\frac{43}{50}$
6. $2\frac{1}{2}$    $\frac{101}{200}$ $3\frac{101}{250}$ $\frac{133}{250}$
7. $7\frac{133}{500}$ $\frac{11}{40}$  $9\frac{227}{500}$ $\frac{211}{250}$
8. $\frac{1}{200}$   $\frac{1}{50}$    $3\frac{9}{10}$  $\frac{1}{125}$

**Page 108**

1. 0.18   8.484  69.726
2. 0.23   6.111  15.161
3. 1.18   16.183 30.408
4. 0.026  1.861  15.773
5. $83.18
6. 33.9 seconds

**Page 109**

1. 9.68    $ 11.64   $ 60.70   187.9    88.267
2. 4.41    $ 27.99   13.35    11.19    $ 7.29
3. 8.718   $ 206.90  $ 63.65  228.010  666.4
4. 21.06   1.90      $ 15.36  7.65     22.396
5. 155.13  67.333    59.88
6. 1.16    11.37     4.989

**Page 110**

1. 1.37     13.48    12.013   54.543   122.218
2. 914.064  171.369  153.703  70.027   48.07
3. 1.29     707.414  495.723  282.793  525.425
4. 254.587  138.281  19.64    9.932    239.163
5. 171.473  105.003  25.127
6. 83.118   245.554  834.243

**Page 111**

1. 5.44     3.26     $ 2.30   4.15    3.24
2. $ 1.54   18.77    369.76   99.06   63.301
3. 19.427   46.701   $ 2.23   29.528  $ 14.21
4. 79.693   7.107    2.092    90.095  7.005
5. $ 11.25  3.152    213.196
6. $ 6.05   $ 10.01  265.441

**Page 112**

(!) 18.79   (A) 18.78    (O) 8.53    (E) 35.65
(N) 180.09  (R) 10.637   (M) 56.95   (P) 48.7
(Y) 5.04    (I) 1.866    (U) 0.17    (S) 47.958
(L) 11.25   (C) 0.92     (D) 68.11   (T) 91.645

Line up your decimals!

**Page 113**

1. $23.74          2. $40.79
3. $74.71          4. a. $46.05  b. 42.5 mph
5. $75.00

**Page 114**

1. 6.81 minutes, yes    2. 11.54 seconds
3. 11.77 seconds        4. Week 1 and 4
5. 42.19 miles          6. 63.89 miles
7. 3.1 meters           8. 3.7 meters

**Page 115**

1. 0.79   9.677   28.347
2. 0.41   6.032   11.165
3. 1.34   11.564  51.438
4. 0.051  1.942   8.715
5. $12.00
6. 45.3 seconds

**Page 116**

1. 2.07    0.48    0.1685  0.5328
2. 0.024   0.009   0.149   0.02202
3. 0.222   2.058   37.74   0.00729
4. 72      48.1    590
5. 64 ounces
6. $2.14

**Page 117**

1. 1596.8   159.68   15.968   159.68   1.5968
2. 1802.4   180.24   18.024   180.24   1.8024
3. 1251.0   125.10   12.510   125.10   1.2510
4. 7.92     2.56     13.09    8.76     69.84
5. 91.14    138.82   172.02   21.142   9.971
6. 65.1472  40.6224  31.2806  86.8042  3.6834

**Page 118**

1. 2.4      2.7      0.84     39.2
2. 13.5     11.24    8.35     18.18
3. 95.2     80.6     240.5    2.38
4. 13.52    4.368    43.472   24.84
5. 535.086  25,115.8 291.928  276.066

Math Connection—Grade 6—RBP0180    www.summerbridgeactivities.com    ©RBP Books

# Answer Pages

## Page 119
| | | | | |
|---|---|---|---|---|
| **1.** | 0.28 | 0.15 | 0.324 | 15.66 |
| **2.** | 5.04 | 0.084 | 0.18 | 0.0264 |
| **3.** | 117.81 | 0.405 | 0.4344 | 0.4002 |
| **4.** | 1.485 | 1.56 | 39.216 | 16.275 |
| **5.** | 2.568 | 58.75 | 22.4536 | 12.9948 |

## Page 120
| | | | | |
|---|---|---|---|---|
| **1.** | 0.00182 | 0.000504 | 0.00387 | 0.001 |
| **2.** | 0.001749 | 0.000672 | 0.00244 | 0.00315 |
| **3.** | 0.0132 | 0.0194 | 0.015 | 0.02451 |
| **4.** | 0.007912 | 0.002875 | 0.003901 | 0.02781 |
| **5.** | 0.000515 | 0.00289 | 0.003552 | 0.000682 |

## Page 121
| | | | |
|---|---|---|---|
| **L** 0.0066 | **Y** 0.066 | **L** 0.094 | **A** 0.0094 |
| **O** 0.00204 | **S** 0.0204 | **I** 0.204 | **C** 2.04 |
| **W** 0.539 | **N** .00539 | **A** 0.005166 | **O** 0.05166 |
| **S** 0.2415 | **A** 0.03192 | **R** 0.00875 | **H** 0.001048 |

They are ALWAYS IN A SCHOOL.

## Page 122
| | | | | |
|---|---|---|---|---|
| **1.** | 6 | 6 | 60 | 6 |
| **2.** | 43 | 430 | 4,300 | 43 |
| **3.** | 653 | 10.9 | 213 | 0.07 |
| **4.** | 46 | 460 | 46 | 4.6 |
| **5.** | 3,900 | 0.045 | 3 | 12,600 |
| **6.** | 123.4 | 110 | 1,100 | 11,000 |

## Page 123
| | | | |
|---|---|---|---|
| **1.** | 2.256 | | |
| | 5 | 2 | 1.6608 |
| **2.** | 7 | 4 | 37.668 |
| | 2 | 3 | 79.36 |
| **3.** | 3 | 2 | 1 | 9.072 |
| | 1 | 7 | 40.23 |
| **4.** | 1 | 1 | 4 | 6.795 |
| | 3 | 6 | 1.9032 |

## Page 124
| | | | |
|---|---|---|---|
| **1.** | 22.5 miles | **2.** | 37.5 pounds |
| **3.** | $4.13 | **4.** | $5.60 |
| **5.** | 42.55 hours | **6.** | $2.31 |
| **7.** | 36.5 meters | **8.** | 23.8 km |

## Page 125
| | | | |
|---|---|---|---|
| **1.** | 63.65 ml | **2.** | 56.096 ml |
| **3.** | 136.8 cm | **4.** | 0.63 kg |
| **5.** | 116.56 calories | **6.** | 2.1 cm |

## Page 126
| | | | | |
|---|---|---|---|---|
| **1.** | 1.26 | .42 | 0.1032 | 2.7004 |
| **2.** | 0.063 | 0.03 | 0.1435 | 0.02778 |
| **3.** | 0.243 | 1.778 | 76.36 | 0.00186 |
| **4.** | 39 | 46.3 | 920 | |
| **5.** | 134 ounces | | | |
| **6.** | 0.036 miles | | | |

## Page 127
| | | | | |
|---|---|---|---|---|
| **1.** | 0.9 | 0.42 | 0.23 | 2.14 |
| **2.** | 8.03 | 5.07 | 0.009 | 0.0063 |
| **3.** | .08 | 2.3 | 230 | 36 |

| | | | | |
|---|---|---|---|---|
| **4.** | 0.418 | 0.605 | 0.0936 | |
| **5.** | 0.12 | 0.875 | 0.144 | 0.625 |
| **6.** | $0.27 | | | |
| **7.** | 12.75 feet | | | |

## Page 128
| | | | | |
|---|---|---|---|---|
| **1.** | 0.3 | 0.03 | 0.23 | 0.023 |
| **2.** | 22.7 | 2.27 | $ 4.91 | 0.021 |
| **3.** | 20.1 | 2.01 | 0.61 | $ 0.46 |
| **4.** | 0.98 | 1.84 | 0.949 | $ 1.30 |
| **5.** | 0.1122 | 8.541 | $ 108.64 | 0.038 |

## Page 129
| | | | | | |
|---|---|---|---|---|---|
| **1.** | 0.54 | 1.15 | 0.95 | 1.825 | 0.3125 |
| **2.** | 0.0775 | 1.62 | 1.575 | 0.146 | 1.05 |
| **3.** | 0.838 | 0.748 | 13.35 | 0.0565 | 15.004 |
| **4.** | 0.535 | 1.34 | 0.325 | 0.2125 | 0.175 |

## Page 130
| | | | | | |
|---|---|---|---|---|---|
| **1.** | 0.7 | 0.08 | 0.009 | 0.07 | 0.016 |
| **2.** | 0.065 | 0.02375 | 0.0902 | 0.01775 | 0.095 |
| **3.** | 0.00625 | 0.03 | 6.24 | 0.006 | 0.013 |
| **4.** | 0.0207 | 0.035 | 3.5 | 0.033 | 0.0085 |

## Page 131
| | | | | |
|---|---|---|---|---|
| **1.** | 9 | 0.2 | 9.9 | 0.8 |
| **2.** | 6.2 | 7 | 0.5 | 0.8 |
| **3.** | 3 | 4.3 | 0.7 | 0.3 |
| **4.** | 2.14 | 0.97 | 0.84 | 0.17 |

## Page 132
| | | | | |
|---|---|---|---|---|
| **1.** | 510 | 50 | 20 | 2000 |
| **2.** | 212.5 | 435 | 595 | 48.75 |
| **3.** | 35 | 34 | 5 | 24 |
| **4.** | 475 | 47.2 | 320 | 180 |
| **5.** | 85 | 8 | 94 | 30 |

## Page 133
| | | | | |
|---|---|---|---|---|
| **1.** | .405 | .0025 | .703 | .003 |
| **2.** | 9.83 | .909 | 45.18 | 386.93 |
| **3.** | 8.856 | .00009 | .00075 | .00057 |
| **4.** | .00703 | 7.441 | .02301 | .32016 |
| **5.** | .9125 | 63.92 | 7.452 | 251.25 |
| **6.** | .4785 | .0235 | .4542 | .3667 |

## Page 134
| | | | | | |
|---|---|---|---|---|---|
| **1.** | .8 | .375 | .6 | .6 | .76 |
| **2.** | .85 | .04 | .225 | .72 | .1875 |
| **3.** | .555 | .3125 | .225 | .32 | .475 |
| **4.** | .75 | .6875 | .5 | .435 | .12 |
| **5.** | .45 | .975 | .375 | .058 | .056 |

## Page 135
| | | | | | |
|---|---|---|---|---|---|
| **1.** | $.66 | **2.** | $.42 | **3.** | $.22 |
| **4.** | $0.04 | **5.** | $.19 | **6.** | $.02 |

## Page 136
| | | | |
|---|---|---|---|
| **1.** | 200 trombones | **2.** | .055 watt |
| **3.** | 28 pianos | **4.** | **a.** 19.14 watts **b.** 6.38 watts |
| **5.** | 11 pianos | **6.** | .08 watt | **7.** 24 watts |

# Answer Pages

## Page 137
1. .6 — .37 — .12 — 1.37
2. 5.09 — 2.03 — .003 — .0037
3. .04 — 1.5 — 180 — 25
4. .418 — .605 — .0936
5. .45 — .1875 — .4 — .136
6. $.49 each
7. 5.8647 grams

## Page 138
1. P = 38 in. — P = 11 ft. — P = 19 m
   A = 90 in.² — A = 7 ft.² — A = 22.5 m²
2. P = 28.5 in. — P = 90 yd. — P = 22 cm
   A = 41 in.² — A = 450 yd.² — A = 27.01 cm²
3. P = 48 in. — P = 36 ft. — P = 102 cm
   A = 104 in.² — A = 45 ft.² — A = 432 cm²

## Page 139
1. 54 — 200 — 13
2. 30 — 48 — 17.5
3. 40 — 90 — 172.2
4. 4.5 cm²
5. 24 ft.²

## Page 140
1. $\frac{5}{7}$  $\frac{20}{13}$
2. $\frac{12}{5}$  $\frac{4}{9}$
3. $\frac{23}{45}$  $\frac{10}{3}$
4. $\frac{1}{4}$  $\frac{3}{25}$
5. $\frac{3}{3}$
6. $\frac{2}{3}$
7. $\frac{3}{3}$
8. $\frac{2}{8}$ or $\frac{1}{4}$
9. $\frac{49}{54}$
10. $\frac{57}{47}$
11. $\frac{42}{104}$
12. $\frac{60}{44}$
13. $\frac{56}{47}$

## Page 141
1. n = 30 — n = 9 — n = 30 — n = 56
2. n = 27
3. n = 40
4. n = 50
5. n = 156
6. n = 40
7. n = 400
8. n = 12
9. n = 240
10. n = 250

## Page 142
1. m = 4 — a = 1 — d = 4 — n = 14
2. p = 18 — j = 2 — s = 20 — y = 9
3. r = 1 — k = 36 — g = 24 — t = 7
4. b = 10 — m = 4 — r = 12 — n = 3
5. s = 24 — f = 15 — v = 120 — s = 4

## Page 143
1. 79% — 5% — 27% — 50%
2. 9% — 80% — 4% — 37%
3. 86% — 150% — 99% — 200%
4. $\frac{50}{100}$ $\frac{33}{100}$ $\frac{65}{100}$ $\frac{56}{100}$ $\frac{30}{100}$ $\frac{5}{100}$ $\frac{98}{100}$ $\frac{7}{100}$
   $\frac{1}{2}$ $\frac{33}{100}$ $\frac{13}{20}$ $\frac{14}{25}$ $\frac{3}{10}$ $\frac{1}{20}$ $\frac{49}{50}$ $\frac{7}{100}$
5. $\frac{10}{100}$ $\frac{60}{100}$ $\frac{90}{100}$ $\frac{75}{100}$ $\frac{10}{100}$ $\frac{60}{100}$ $\frac{50}{100}$ $\frac{2}{100}$ $\frac{65}{100}$
   10% 60% 90% 75% 10% 60% 50% 2% 65%

## Page 144
1. 2% — 6% — 1% — 8%
2. 10% — 20% — 12% — 24%
3. 37% — 69% — 40% — 21%
4. 75% — 70% — 25% — 50%
5. 99.9% — 49.9% — 175% — 225%
6. .24 — .65 — .88 — .03
7. .17 — .09 — .1 — .86
8. .75 — .2 — .04 — .5
9. .3 — .9 — .05 — .12
10. .667 — .333 — 1.45 — 2.1

## Page 145
1. .02 — 2%
2. $\frac{3}{100}$ — .03
3. $\frac{3}{25}$ — 12%
4. .375 — 37.5%
5. $\frac{7}{20}$ — 35%
6. $\frac{9}{20}$ — 45%
7. $\frac{1}{2}$ — .5
8. .72 — 72%
9. $\frac{9}{10}$ — .9
10. 1
    ninety-nine percent
11. a. 7th grade    b. 8th grade

## Page 146
1. .3 — 1.2 — 12.8 — 9
2. 6.48 — 4.8 — 8.1 — 4.84
3. 5.44 — 6.75 — 38.44 — 33.44
4. 16 — 6 — 18.87 — 12.04
5. 2.46 — 14.3 — 180 — 50
6. 36 — 60 — 500 — 270

## Page 147
1. $9.60 — $14.40    2. $7.50 — $17.50
3. $12.00 — $68.00    4. $132.00 — $88.00
5. $49.50 — $40.50    6. $54.00 — $66.00
7. $312.50 — $937.50    8. $99.00 — $99.00
9. $9.75 — $55.25    10. $1.60 — $2.40
11. $8.00 — $72.00    12. $7.00 — $13.00
13. $1.20 — $4.80    14. $32.67 — $66.33

## Page 148
1. 60%    2. 150 grams    3. 244 milk jugs
4. a. $\frac{3}{4}$
   b. 0.75
   c. 75%
5. $62.40
6. a. $\frac{3}{4}$
   b. For every 3 baths, you can take 4 showers

## Page 149
1. 4.1    2. 143
3. Perimeter = 95.8 yards    Area = 519.58 square yards
4. Perimeter = 320 yards    Area = 6,000 square yards
5. 5,480.42 square yards
6. Mean 11; Median 10; Mode 5
7. 200 times

## Page 150
1. $\frac{7}{10}$    2. $\frac{7}{20}$    3. $\frac{19}{20}$
4. $\frac{1}{20}$    5. 59.5 pounds    6. 28.28 quarts
7. $\frac{1}{50}$    8. 6.8 pounds    9. 96 calories

Math Connection—Grade 6—RBP0180
www.summerbridgeactivities.com
© RBP Books